LIFE-SIZE

SHARKS
KILLER CREATURES
REPTILES

STERLING

New York / London
www.sterlingpublishing.com/kids

Material first published in the UK by Pavilion Children's Books,
an imprint of Anova Books plc,
10 Southcombe Street, London, W14 0RA

Life-Size Sharks
Text copyright © 2005 Daniel Gilpin
Concept © 2004 David Bergen

Life-Size Killer Creatures
Copyright © 2006 Anova Books Company Ltd

Life-Size Reptiles
Copyright © 2007 by Anova Books plc
Text copright © 2007 Anova Books plc
Concept copyright © 2004 David Bergen
Picture Credits: page 122, Photos.com

Library of Congress Cataloging-in-Publication Date Available

10 9 8 7 6 5 4 3 2 1

Life-Size
First Published in 2007 by
Sterling Publishing Co., Inc.
387 Park Avenue South
New York, NY 10016

Distributed in Canada by
Sterling Publishing
c/o Canadian Manda Group
165 Dufferin Street
Toronto, Canada M6K 3H6

ISBN-13: 978-1-4027-5944-4
ISBN-10: 1-4027-5944-4

LIFE-SIZE

SHARKS

and other

UNDERWATER CREATURES

WRITTEN BY
DANIEL GILPIN

ILLUSTRATED BY
MARTIN KNOWELDEN

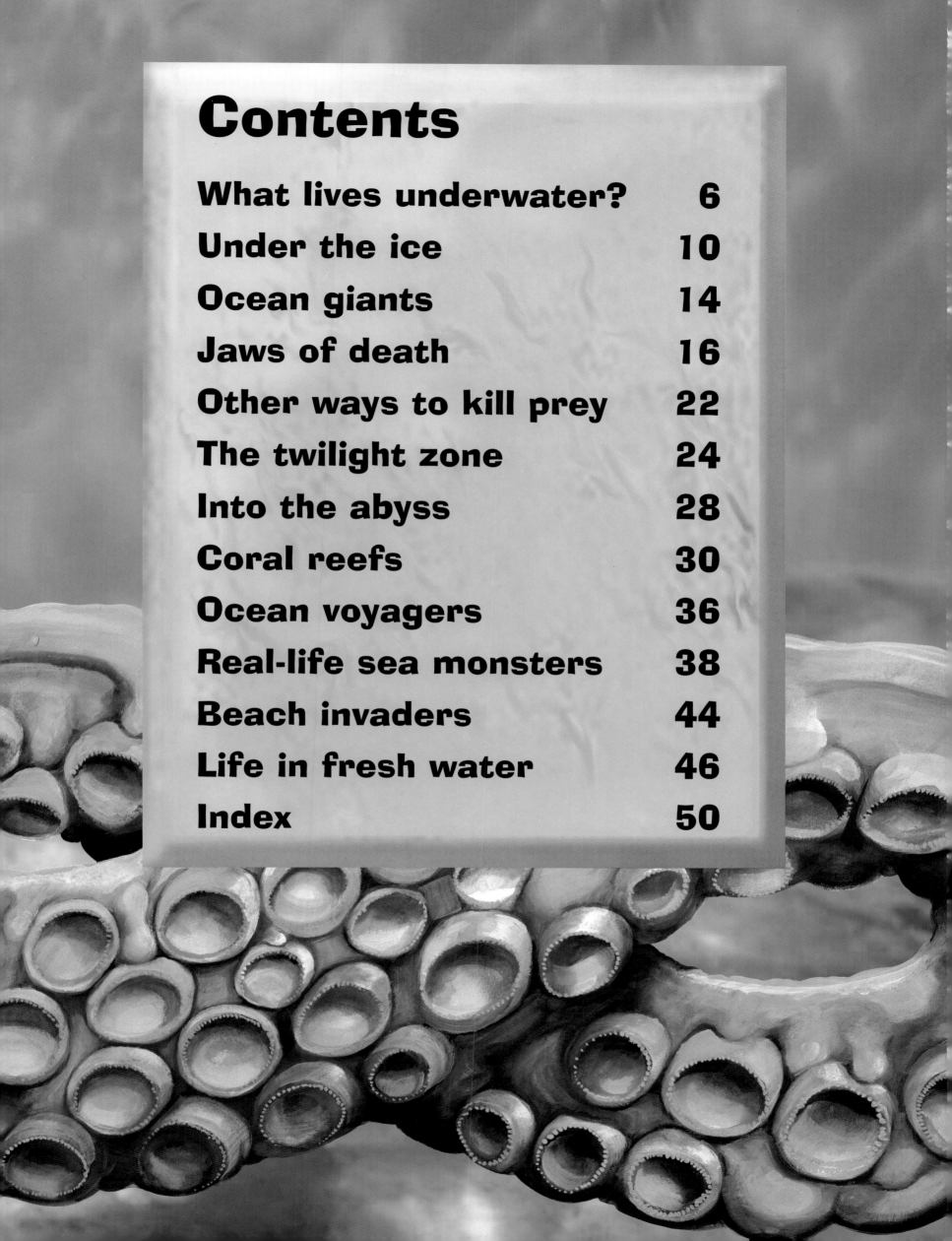

Contents

Voyages of discovery

Most of the ocean is still unexplored. Many of the creatures that live down there have never been seen by human eyes. Each time scientists send submarines into the deep sea, they are going on voyages of discovery. New types of animal are being found there all the time, and some of them are very strange indeed.

In 2001, a new type of squid was discovered, with giant fins and stiff arms that stick out like the spokes of a bicycle wheel. Two years later, a weird type of armored snail covered in plates made of iron minerals was found.

Black-banded sea krait

The Life-size stamp

This stamp shows which sharks and other underwater creatures are illustrated as life size in this book. It's just as surprising to see how tiny things are, like the seahorse on this page, as to see how big they are. It's not possible to show all the creatures life size—the blue whale on page 12 is so big that its eye would barely fit into one page of this book! When creatures are not shown life size, a hand print, or human diver is included to give a sense of scale.

The deadly black-banded sea krait spends most of its time in warm water around coral reefs. Its tail is flattened to make a paddle. Sea kraits often slither onto land to lay eggs, find mates and to warm up in the sunshine.

WHAT LIVES UNDERWATER?

Water covers more than two thirds of our planet. Almost all of it is contained in the world's oceans and seas, and a huge number of animals live underwater. Some are familiar to most of us, but many are little known and hardly ever seen.

Fish and other vertebrates

Vertebrates are animals that have backbones, like us. Fish are vertebrates, and so are mammals and reptiles. Most underwater vertebrates are fish. Unlike mammals and reptiles, which must breathe air, fish breathe by removing oxygen from the water using organs called gills. More than 27,500 species (types) of fish have been discovered so far. They range in size from the tiny, ⅓-inch (9 mm) long dwarf goby to the whale shark, which can reach 59 feet (18 m) long.

Mammals that live underwater include seals, whales and dolphins. Underwater reptiles include turtles, crocodiles and sea snakes.

Seahorses must be some of the most unusual-looking fish. They feed on tiny floating animals, which they suck in through their tube-shaped mouths.

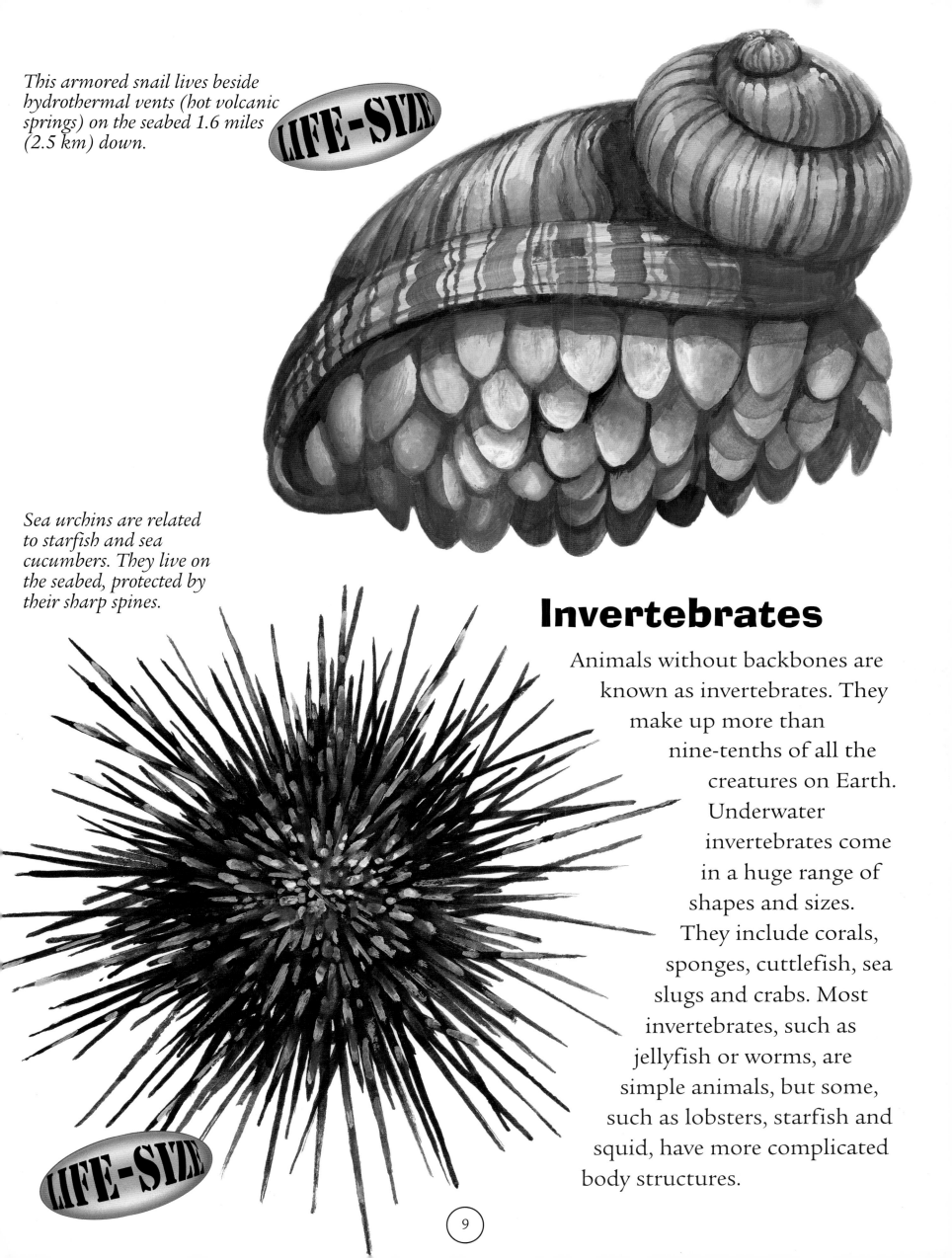

This armored snail lives beside hydrothermal vents (hot volcanic springs) on the seabed 1.6 miles (2.5 km) down.

LIFE-SIZE

Sea urchins are related to starfish and sea cucumbers. They live on the seabed, protected by their sharp spines.

LIFE-SIZE

Invertebrates

Animals without backbones are known as invertebrates. They make up more than nine-tenths of all the creatures on Earth. Underwater invertebrates come in a huge range of shapes and sizes. They include corals, sponges, cuttlefish, sea slugs and crabs. Most invertebrates, such as jellyfish or worms, are simple animals, but some, such as lobsters, starfish and squid, have more complicated body structures.

UNDER THE ICE

Much of the ocean around the North and South Poles is covered by ice. The creatures that live under it have to be especially tough to survive, yet large numbers manage to do so, including the world's biggest whales.

Krill

The most common animals in Antarctic waters (around the South Pole) are krill. These shrimplike creatures feed on tiny plantlike algae, which grow on the ice and in the sea itself. In spring and summer, krill form vast swarms, containing millions of individuals. Scientists think that there are around five hundred thousand billion krill in the oceans. That means that for every person on the planet there are more than eighty thousand krill! Krill are extremely important animals in the Antarctic, as they are eaten by almost all of the larger creatures that live there, from penguins to whales.

Krill may live for up to six years, if they can escape being eaten.

LIFE-SIZE

...ic whales

...mer, the Arctic Ocean is full of whales. Many kinds, such as humpbacks
...ay whales, swim up from seas farther south to feed on the huge shoals of
...hat appear in the Arctic at this time of year.

...w types of whale spend their whole lives in the Arctic Ocean. They include
... bowhead whale, a 110-ton (100 metric tonnes) giant that has the biggest
...outh of any animal on Earth—fully open, it could swallow
... minivan! More common
...residents include the smaller
beluga whale and narwhal.

Narwal

Beluga

Bowhead

These three species live in Arctic waters all year round.

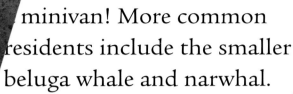

LIFE-SIZE

Many polar fish have special adaptations to help them survive. For instance, the Antarctic ice fish has a natural antifreeze in its blood to prevent it freezing up.

Coping with cold

The sea creatures that live around the Arctic and Antarctic have different ways of dealing with the cold. Most air-breathing animals, such as whales, have a thick layer of fat just beneath the skin. This layer, known as blubber, acts like a blanket, keeping their body heat in.

Unlike whales, fish do not have blubber. Instead, they let their bodies get very cold. Polar fish save energy by being less active than fish in warmer waters. They don't get eaten because predatory fish are less active, too. However, hot-blooded, air-breathing animals, such as seals and penguins, find it easy to catch them!

Greenland shark

The Arctic Ocean (around the North Pole) has its own terrifying predator—the Greenland, or sleeper, shark. At 21 feet (6.5 m) long, this monster is the world's fourth largest shark—only the whale shark, basking shark and great white shark are bigger. Drifting along slowly to save its energy, the sleeper shark bursts into action when it sights prey. It eats almost anything, from fast-moving salmon to the flesh of dead whales. One Greenland shark was even found to have a whole reindeer in its stomach!

OCEAN GIANTS

The seas are home to the planet's biggest creatures. Animals can grow much larger here than on land because the water supports their bodies. Whales, the largest creatures of all, are mammals and must breathe air.

Filter-feeders

The world's biggest animals have enormous appetites. But rather than hunt other large animals, most eat huge amounts of much smaller prey. The world's three biggest whales—the blue whale, fin whale and bowhead—all feed on fish or krill. They gulp great mouthfuls of sea water filled with their tiny prey. The whales then filter this water through comblike curtains called baleen plates that line their mouths. Other giant filter-feeders, such as whale sharks and manta rays, eat even smaller sea life, known as plankton. They use their gills to sieve this food from the water.

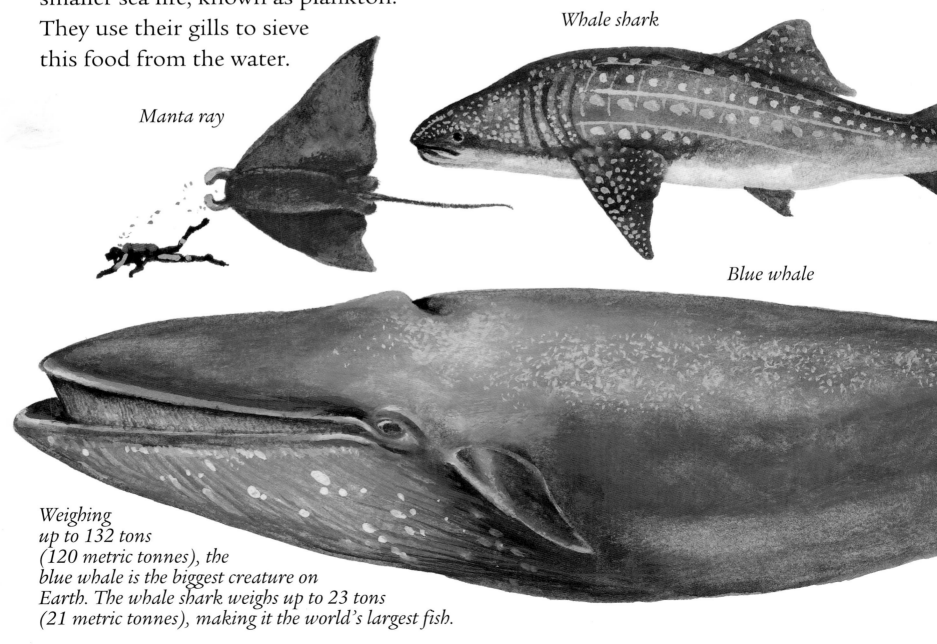

Whale shark

Manta ray

Blue whale

Weighing up to 132 tons (120 metric tonnes), the blue whale is the biggest creature on Earth. The whale shark weighs up to 23 tons (21 metric tonnes), making it the world's largest fish.

Cooperative killers

The killer whale is one of the most ferocious animals in the ocean. It hunts and kills all sorts of prey, including the blue whale and other creatures bigger than itself. Killer whales live and travel in family groups. They are highly intelligent and often work together to catch their food. Adult male killer whales can grow up to 27 feet (8 m) long and weigh 10 tons (9 metric tonnes). The females are smaller, usually reaching about 20 feet (6 m) long and weighing less than 6 ½ tons (6 metric tonnes).

The giant squid may weigh up to 2 ⅛ tons (2 metric tonnes), but it is little match for a 55-ton (50 metric tonnes) sperm whale.

The world's biggest predator

Although most of the world's great whales feed on small prey, there is one that takes on animals nearer its own size. The sperm whale is the world's fifth largest animal and its favorite food is another monster, the giant squid.

Sperm whales can dive to enormous depths. Occasionally, they may swim down as far as 2 miles (3 km) beneath the surface in search of prey. Sperm whales must hold their breath for an extremely long time, sometimes spending two hours underwater before coming up for air.

JAWS OF DEATH

The sea's most dangerous creatures can kill with a single bite. Sharks bite chunks from their prey, so that it quickly bleeds to death. They attack suddenly, powering into their victims before they have time to react.

Tiger shark

Bull shar

Great white shark

The great white shark (botto... world's most dangerous shar... tiger shark (top) and bull sha... also eat people.

Man-eating sharks

Most sharks are harmless but some kill and eat people! T... fearsome of all sharks is the great white. Its usual prey are... but on a few occasions it mistakes swimmers or surfers fo... More than 250 people have been attacked by great white s... over the last few hundred years, and nearly 70 have been ... Other man-eaters include the tiger shark, bull shark, requ... shark and shortfin mako. In all, sharks attack about 100 ... people every year, and about a quarter of their victims d...

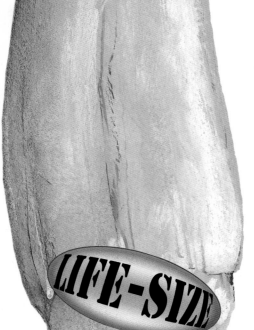

LIFE-SIZE

A new set of gnashers

Sharks are constantly growing new teeth. As old ones come loose or wear out, they are replaced by a new, sharper set behind them. Sharks use their teeth for slicing and ripping up flesh. Some may get through as many as 25,000 in a lifetime.

Fearsome fish

It is not just sharks that attack humans. All sorts of other fish can give a nasty bite if they feel threatened. One of the worst reputations belongs to the barracuda. This fast-moving predator usually keeps its distance but might turn on divers that have chased it or drifted too close.

The moray eel is another fish with a fierce reputation. It lives in warm seas and grows to 10 feet (3 m) long. By day, it hides in cracks and crevices among coral or rocks. If startled, it will lunge forward with its jaws open and bite anything that does not retreat.

Moray eels are fish with round snakelike bodies.

The barracuda is one of the most streamlined of all fish. When it swims, its body cuts through the water like a knife.

Head of a barracuda

LIFE-SIZE

Mega bites

The great white is the biggest predatory shark in the sea, growing to at least 23 feet (7 m) long, maybe bigger. But it would have been small fry compared to its extinct cousin *megalodon*. This gigantic hunter is thought to have reached at least 50 feet (15 m) in length. Its huge teeth make those of the great white shark look puny! Most sharks' teeth have serrated (sawlike) edges to help them cut through flesh. Steak knives have serrated blades for exactly the same reason.

LIFE-SIZE

Even the most unlikely creatures can be poisonous. The cone shell shoots its prey with a hollow spike, through which poison is injected.

OTHER WAYS TO KILL PREY

A swift attack and powerful bite is just one way to kill prey. Many underwater creatures use less obvious methods. Some lie in wait for prey, hidden by camouflage. Others draw their victims toward their mouths by using bait.

Hidden dangers

Not all predators travel in search of prey, some wait for their victims to come to them. These are the ambush specialists—animals that stay hidden, waiting for the right moment to strike.

Most ambushers rely on camouflage to avoid being seen. They are colored, and sometimes even shaped, to match their surroundings. Stonefish, for instance, look almost exactly like the rocks on the seabed where they live. Their relatives, scorpionfish, are often colored to blend in with seaweed.

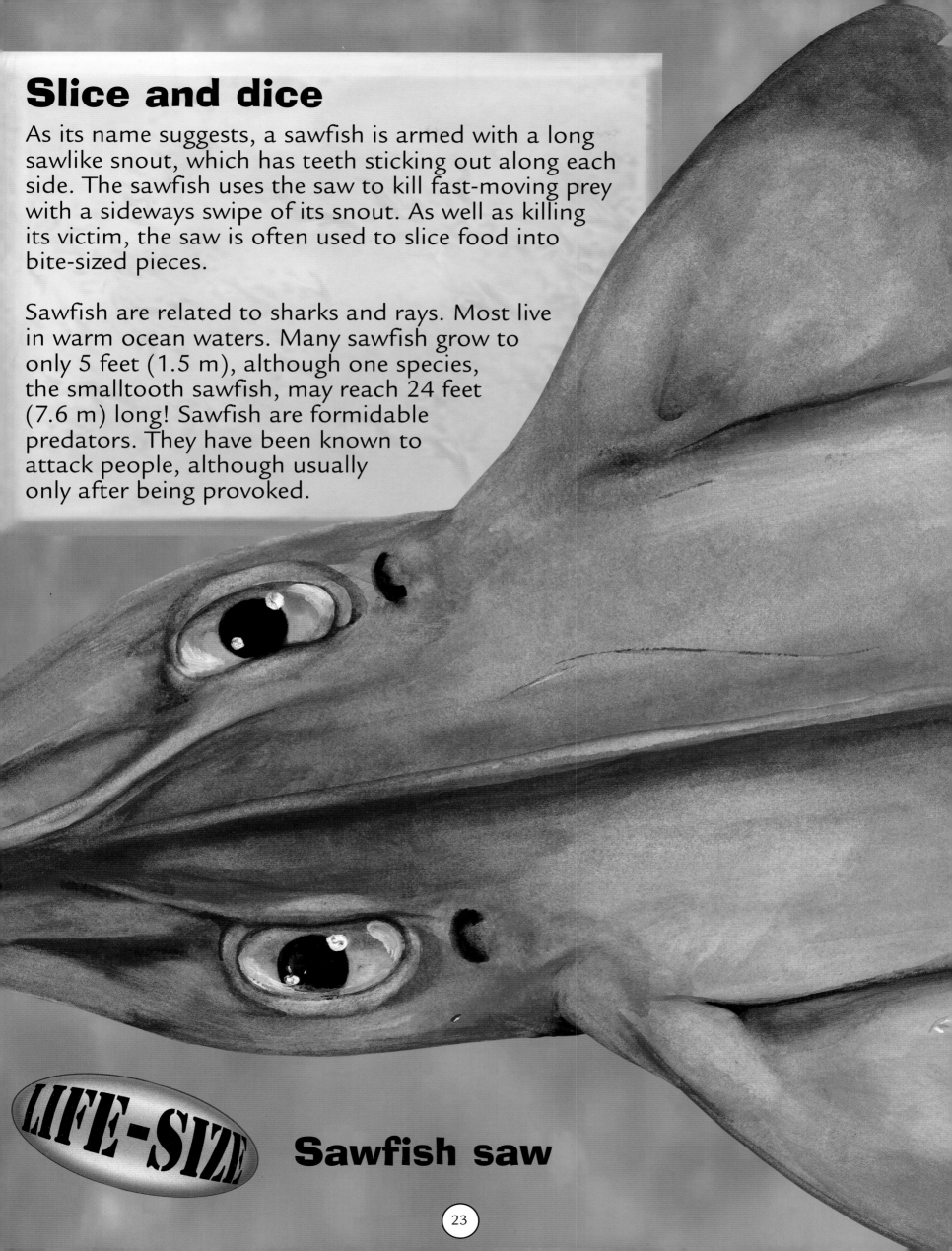

Slice and dice

As its name suggests, a sawfish is armed with a long sawlike snout, which has teeth sticking out along each side. The sawfish uses the saw to kill fast-moving prey with a sideways swipe of its snout. As well as killing its victim, the saw is often used to slice food into bite-sized pieces.

Sawfish are related to sharks and rays. Most live in warm ocean waters. Many sawfish grow to only 5 feet (1.5 m), although one species, the smalltooth sawfish, may reach 24 feet (7.6 m) long! Sawfish are formidable predators. They have been known to attack people, although usually only after being provoked.

LIFE-SIZE

Sawfish saw

THE TWILIGHT ZONE

Between 500 and 2,300 feet (152 and 701 m) below the ocean's surface, the amount of light reaching through the water gradually fades. Known as the twilight zone, this habitat has its own unique animals, many unlike anything else on Earth.

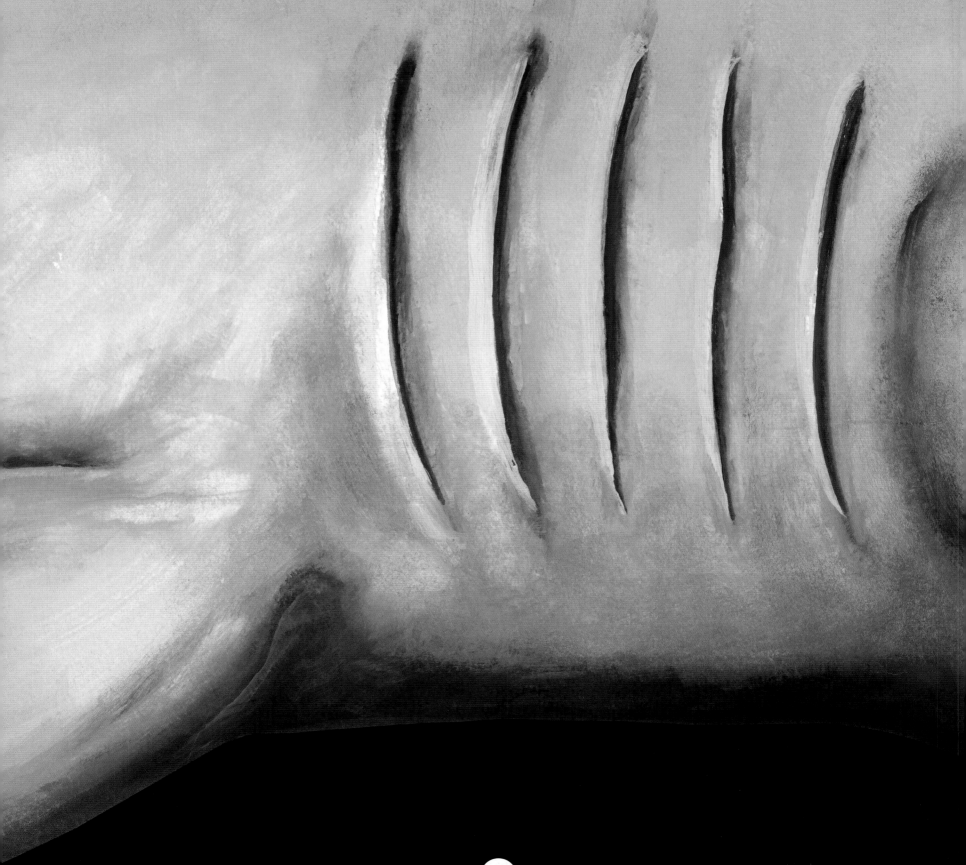

ɔwing in the gloom

ɔ little sunshine reaches down into the
dight zone. But surprisingly this part of
ɪe ocean is sometimes lit with another type
ɔf light. Many twilight-zone animals are able
to produce their own light.
Some do this to tell mates
where they are. Others do
it to catch prey. Anglerfish,
for example, have luminous
lures to draw prey toward their
mouths. There is even one fish
that generates light for camouflage.
Called the hatchet fish, it has two
rows of lights on its belly, which
match the color of sunlight
coming down from above.

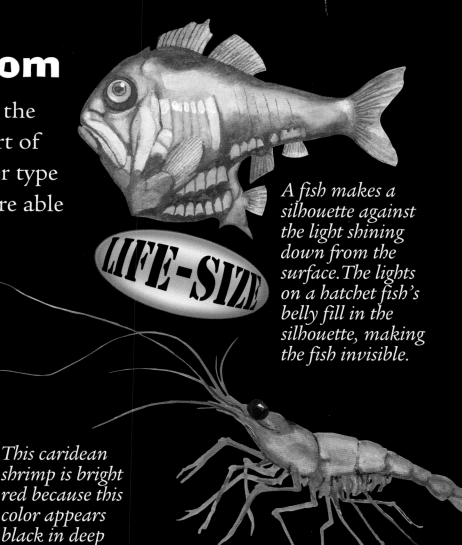

A fish makes a silhouette against the light shining down from the surface. The lights on a hatchet fish's belly fill in the silhouette, making the fish invisible.

This caridean shrimp is bright red because this color appears black in deep water, making it hard to see.

Fishing for food

Anglerfish use bait to attract their prey just like people do when
they go fishing. But instead of a fishing rod, an anglerfish has a
long spine that sticks out from its head. On the end of the spine
is a fleshy lure that looks to many fish like a piece of food. The
anglerfish twitches this lure to attract small fish into its large,
toothy mouth. Anglerfish that live in deep and dark waters use
lures that glow in
the dark.

Anglerfish have fearsome teeth that are used to stab their prey and make sure it does not get away.

Twilight nightmare

Few fish look more frightening than the goblin shark. This bizarre bottom-dwelling monster has a face that would terrify even the toughest diver. Unlike other sharks, it has a long, flattened snout and jaws that it can push out of its mouth. This helps it to snap up prey quickly.

The goblin shark spends most of its time in the dark water near the seabed. Its tiny eyes see very little. However, the shark's long snout is equipped with electricity sensors that help it find prey on or even buried under the seabed. The goblin shark lives mostly in coastal waters where the seabed slopes gradually downward away from the shore. It hunts squid, fish and other creatures living near the sea bottom. The shark even catches crabs, crushing their shells in its back teeth. Male goblin sharks reach 12 ½ feet (3.8 m) long.

LIFE-SIZE

INTO THE ABYSS

Below 2,300 feet (700 m), the ocean is cold and completely dark. This forbidding place is the deep sea, and it is home to some of the weirdest and most scary-looking of all underwater creatures.

Drifting in darkness

Deep-sea animals inhabit a world without sunlight. Some live on the seabed, but many float freely in the still, dark water, never seeing and rarely feeling a solid surface.

Many free-swimming animals in the deep sea have soft, fragile bodies. Comb jellies, for instance, are more than nine-tenths water! Others have tougher but often still flexible bodies. The vampire squid, for example, has powerful muscles that can change its body shape at will.

Adult vampire squid have earlike fins, which they flap up and down to move themselves through the water.

Super senses

In the blackness of the deep sea, eyesight becomes unimportant and other senses take over. One of the most important of these is touch and the ability to sense vibrations and currents in the water. The hairy anglerfish has long, fleshy hairs covering its body. These pick up the slightest movement and direct the fish toward its prey.

Another important sense in the deep sea is smell. Sharks have a highly developed sense of smell. Deep-sea species, such as the bluntnose sixgill shark, use it to find the rotting bodies of dead animals that have sunk to the ocean floor.

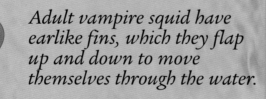

Hunting in the dark

Catching prey in complete darkness is very difficult. To improve their chances of hitting victims, many deep-sea predators have long, protruding teeth. The viperfish has some of the most frightening teeth of all. They stick out from its mouth like long, curved needles, ready to impale any creature that comes into reach.

Some deep-sea hunters have small teeth but huge mouths. One of the most extreme examples is the gulper eel. This 6-foot (1.8 m) animal has such a huge mouth that it hardy ever misses. Prey is snapped up in its pelicanlike jaws, which can unhinge to grab fish as big as the eel itself.

Staying out of sight

Animals living in open water have no place to hide. Many survive by keeping an eye out for danger and they make a very quick getaway when hunters approach.

Other sea animals, such as jellyfish and shrimp, avoid attacks by being transparent. What little light does come from above passes right through their bodies, making them almost invisible.

Viper fish

Like many deep-sea fish, the viper fish has a large stomach that can expand, allowing it to eat a lot whenever food is plentiful.

LIFE-SIZE

Hammerhead
shark

CORAL REEFS

Coral reefs are sometimes called the rainforests of the sea. Like rainforests, the reefs are home to a huge range of animals. The biodiversity of a coral reef is higher than any other part of the ocean. This means that more different types of plant and animal live here than anywhere else.

Bright and beautiful

Coral-reef fish are among the most colorful creatures on Earth. They come in nearly every color imaginable. Some are so bright that they almost glow. The reason for these rainbow colors is hard to understand. They certainly do not help the fish hide from predators! Scientists think that they might simply be a way for fish to identify others of their own kind in the crowded waters.

Coral-reef fish include angelfish and butterfly fish. Angelfish munch on sponges, while butterfly fish eat tiny worms and swimming animals.

LIFE-SIZE

Imperial angelfish

Forceps butterfly fish

How corals live

Corals are colonies of many small animals, known as polyps. Each polyp looks like a tiny sea anemone, with a ring of stinging tentacles around its mouth. Many coral polyps produce a hard, chalky case around their bodies to protect them from predators. The protective cases of polyps in colonies grow together to form beautiful structures. When a polyp dies, its skeleton is left behind, and a new polyp grows on top of it. Coral polyps are animals, but many have tiny plantlike algae living inside them. Whenever sunlight shines on these algae, they produce sugars, which they share with the polyp.

Over many thousands of years, the chalky cases left behind by coral polyps build up to produce the massive underwater structures we call coral reefs.

Living together

Some coral-reef creatures live in partnerships. Clownfish live among the tentacles of sea anemones, for example. The tentacles keep predators away from the clownfish. Slime on the fish's skin protects it from the anemone's stings.

The cleaner wrasse has a partnership with many types of coral-reef animal. Instead of attacking the little fish, they let it swim all over them, even into their mouths. The wrasse nips off parasites from the other creatures' bodies. (Parasites are animals that live on or inside the body of another animal.) Everyone benefits from this system. The larger fish get rid of their pests while the cleaner wrasse gets a meal.

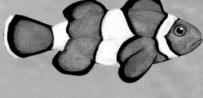

Clownfish are often also called anemonefish because of the way they live alongside large sea anemones.

Wide-eyed

The great hammerhead shark is one of the most deadly of all coral-reef hunters. With its huge mouth and razor-sharp teeth, this 20-foot (6 m) monster can make mincemeat of any animal it decides to attack.

Like all hammerheads, the great hammerhead has its eyes, nostrils and other sense organs wide apart. It may be that this helps the shark to find its prey. Having its eyes far apart might help the hammerhead judge distances better. Its nostrils are widely spaced too, and this could make it easier for the shark to detect in which direction a particular smell is coming from. As with all sharks, hammerheads can also sense the electricity produced by another animal's muscles. The hammer-shaped head also makes this sense more accurate.

OCEAN VOYAGERS

Compared to shallow, coastal waters, the open ocean is almost completely empty of life, like a desert on land. The few animals that do live out there have special adaptations to help them survive. Many of them travel across the open ocean on long journeys, known as migrations.

Going with the flow

Many open-ocean animals drift along with the current. Jellyfish move by pulsing their bell-shaped bodies, but they cannot swim very well. Instead, they travel wherever the ocean waters take them and catch food with stinging tentacles that trail below. Another ocean drifter is the Portuguese man-of-war. It is actually made up of hundreds of animals living together. Some of them form a large, air-filled float, which has a sail to catch the wind. Others make up stinging tentacles to trap prey and another group break down food.

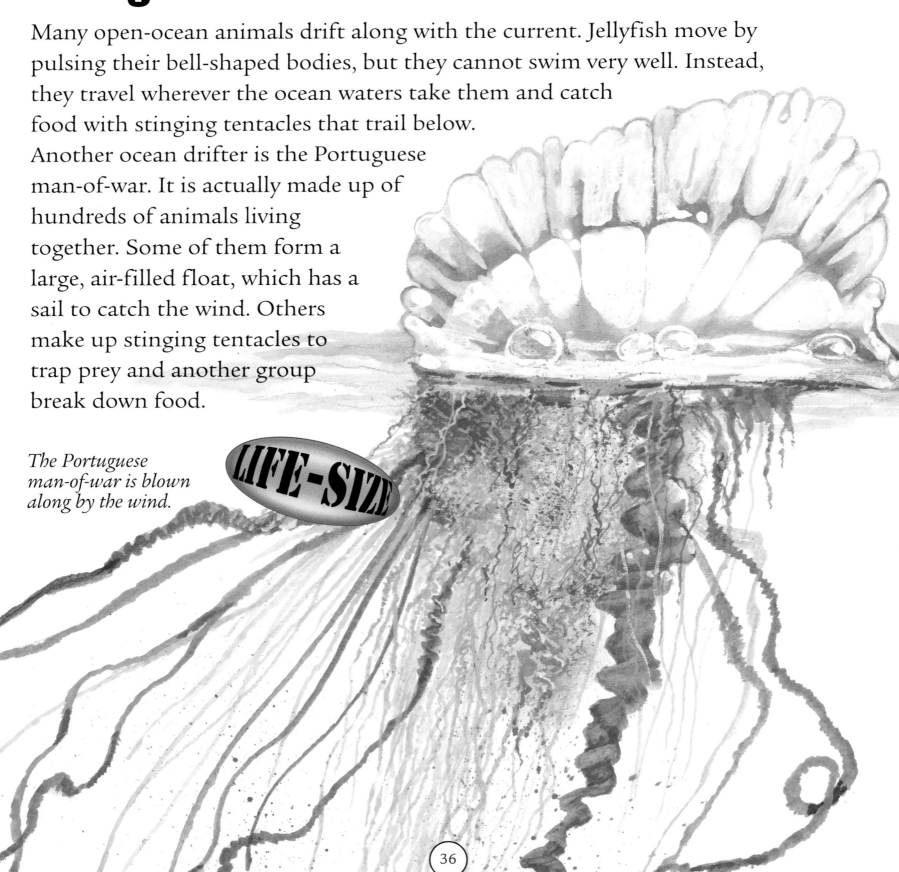

The Portuguese man-of-war is blown along by the wind.

LIFE-SIZE

Sprint finishers

In the open ocean there is nowhere to hide. The fish that live here are fast swimmers and can see danger coming from a long way off. For predators to survive, they have to be even faster. Open-ocean predators include the quickest animals in the sea. The fastest swimmer of all is the cosmopolitan sailfish. This super-streamlined hunter can reach up to 68 miles per hour (109 kph) in short bursts. Other speedy ocean predators include the shortfin mako shark, which reaches speeds of 60 miles per hour (97 kph) and the marlin, which can swim at 50 miles per hour (81 kph).

The world's fastest swimmer, the cosmopolitan sailfish, grows to 10 feet (3 m) long.

Incredible journey

If it could speak, the common eel would have an amazing story to tell. Although it spends most of its life in the rivers and marshes of Europe, it was born thousands of miles away in the open ocean. When they become adults, common eels leave their freshwater homes and swim down to the sea. They then travel right across the Atlantic Ocean to an area east of the Caribbean, known as the Sargasso Sea. Here, they breed and lay their eggs at the bottom of deep ocean trenches. The adult eels then die, leaving their young to hatch and make the return journey alone.

The common eel swims all the way across the Atlantic Ocean to breed.

The Kraken

Long ago, Vikings told tales of the Kraken. This mighty beast was like a floating island and had tentacles that could pull whole ships underwater. The Kraken was probably more than a myth. Its description matches the giant squid, a true monster that sometimes rises from the deep to swim at the surface. Vikings on the ocean at night may have seen this gigantic creature, which has tentacles 40 feet (12 m) long!

REAL-LIFE SEA MONSTERS

Many tales of sea monsters are based in fact, inspired by sightings of real-life animals. New finds keep adding to our list of monstrous sea creatures. It seems likely that many others might be out there, still waiting to be discovered.

Ancient accounts of real animals inspired stories of monsters. The creature above was drawn from a description of a sawfish.

Oarfish usually live in deep water, but they are occasionally seen swimming near the surface.

Sea serpents

Stories of sea serpents terrified early sailors. Some said that these enormous monsters would reach out and pluck men from the masts and rigging, or wrap their coils around entire ships and drag them under the water.

In truth neither of these things ever happened, but sailors probably did see real creatures they thought were sea serpents. The oarfish, for instance, could definitely be mistaken for a giant sea snake. Its long, slender body grows to a length of 56 feet (17 m).

The basking shark feeds on tiny animals near the surface. It may also bask in the sun on the surface of the water.

Modern sea monsters

Many other sea monsters of old were probably based on sailors seeing real animals, such as whales and sharks. As sailors told each other their stories, these sea creatures became more monstrous and terrifying. Today, we know much more about sea creatures than we did in the past. Seeing a basking shark or a whale shark, the two largest fish in the world, for example, would have struck fear into sailors many years ago. Instead of being ship-sinking monsters, we know today that these sharks are harmless filter-feeders.

The basking shark is about 30 feet (9 m) long and the whale shark grows to an even larger size. Both sharks often float, or bask, on the surface, forming a living island. They even let people walk up and down their backs.

Leviathans

The word *leviathan* is an ancient one. It appears in the Old Testament of the Bible and some even earlier writings. In medieval times, a leviathan was a particular type of giant monster that swam around ships to create whirlpools that sucked them and their crew underwater.

The legend of the leviathan was most probably inspired by sightings of whales. Humpback whales even behave a bit like these monsters, swimming in circles to create rings of bubbles. They use these bubbles to trap fish before bursting up through the middle to swallow their catch.

Humpback whales create 'nets' of bubbles to trap shoals of fish.

Giant-squid tentacles

LIFE-SIZE

BEACH INVADERS

Some sea creatures occasionally come out onto land. Most do this to lay eggs or give birth to their young, but a few actually feed along the shoreline. Many other types of animals that live in coastal waters become trapped in rock pools as the tide goes out.

Mudskipper males raise their dorsal (back) fins to warn rival males to stay away. They scan for danger with eyes that move independently of each other.

LIFE-SIZE

Fish out of water

Mudskippers spend much of their time on land. Like other fish, they have gills to breathe underwater, but they can also take oxygen in through their skin. Mudskippers live along muddy shores in warm regions, from Africa in the west through Asia to the South Pacific. They eat worms and other small creatures that live on the shore.

Mudskippers have adaptations to help them move about on land. Their front fins are strong enough to lift their bodies off the ground, and their muscular tails flick to help them "skip" along. The fish also have a sucker disc on the underside on the body, allowing them to cling to the trunks of mangrove trees, which grow in the shallows.

Coming ashore

Turtles spend most of their lives in the ocean. But every year, females gather to haul themselves onto sandy beaches to lay their eggs. The turtles usually come ashore in darkness. Sometimes hundreds of turtles will arrive on the same beach at one time, churning up the sand with their flippers as they dig pits to bury their eggs in.

Many other air-breathing creatures, such as penguins and seals, come ashore to breed, but, amazingly, there is one type of fish that does it too. Capelin surge up onto beaches with the waves at high tide. The females lay their eggs and the males fertilize them. Then all the adults die. A few weeks later, the baby capelin hatch in the sand. When the next high tide comes in, the baby fish swim out to sea.

Hawksbill turtles may lay 200 eggs at a time. Once they have emerged from the sand, the little hatchlings race down to the sea as fast as their flippers will carry them.

LIFE-SIZE

LIFE-SIZE

Rock pools

All sorts of animals end up in rock pools. As the tide comes in, many creatures that live in the sea come with it and stay behind when the tide goes out. The animals found in rock pools range from crabs and shrimp to sea slugs and small fish. A few, such as barnacles and sea anemones, may spend their whole lives there. Others escape into open water again as soon as they can.

In some parts of the world, rock pools hide dangerous animals. For example, people in Australia often find the small but deadly blue-ringed octopus in pools.

The beautiful but deadly blue-ringed octopus expands its rings as a warning to show that it is poisonous.

LIFE IN FRESH WATER

Freshwater habitats include rivers, lakes, ponds and swamps. The creatures that live there are different from those found in the seas and oceans. Many, however, are just as frightening, dangerous or weird.

Freshwater giants

Most of the world's biggest fish live in the oceans, but a few giants make their home in lakes or rivers. One of the largest freshwater fish is the arapaima, which lives in the Amazon and other South American rivers. It can weigh 440 pounds (200 kg) and reach more than 10 feet (3 m) long!

The alligator snapping turtle is another giant. This monstrous reptile is well named because it has a bite powerful enough to slice its prey in two. The alligator snapper entices fish toward its jaws by wiggling a wormlike lure in the bottom of its opened mouth. Lying in wait on the bottom of a swamp or river, the turtle can be surprisingly well hidden— alligator snappers move about so little that plants often grow on their shells.

The alligator snapper is the world's largest freshwater turtle. The biggest one ever recorded weighed 236 pounds (107 kg).

LIFE-SIZE

Some freshwater turtles grow no bigger than the palm of your hand.

...fish

...piranhas have a bloodthirsty reputation. ...uth American fish can strip the flesh from ...horse in minutes, leaving nothing but the ...ton behind.

...ed-bellied piranhas live and feed in shoals. Once one attacks, the rest quickly follow. The shoal then goes into a feeding frenzy, leaving a victim little hope of escape. Individual red-bellied piranhas are quite small—just 12 inches (30 cm) long—but their shoals may be hundreds strong. These terrifying fish are armed with some of the sharpest teeth of any animal. The teeth are triangles with saw-toothed edges, like those of sharks.

LIFE-SIZE

The red-bellied piranha has a mouthful of razor-sharp teeth.

High voltage

Almost as famous as the red-bellied piranha is South America's electric eel. This river fish eats meat and some grow to 9 feet (2.7 m) long. It uses electricity to stun or kill its prey, firing off shocks of up to 650 volts! That is nearly three times what comes out of a plug at home.

The electric eel can generate a shock large enough to kill a person.

The electric eel's body works like a giant battery. Its muscles generate a powerful electric current, giving the head a negative charge and the tail a positive one. The eel attacks prey by touching them with its head and tail end at the same time. This causes current to run through the prey's body, giving it a deadly electric shock.

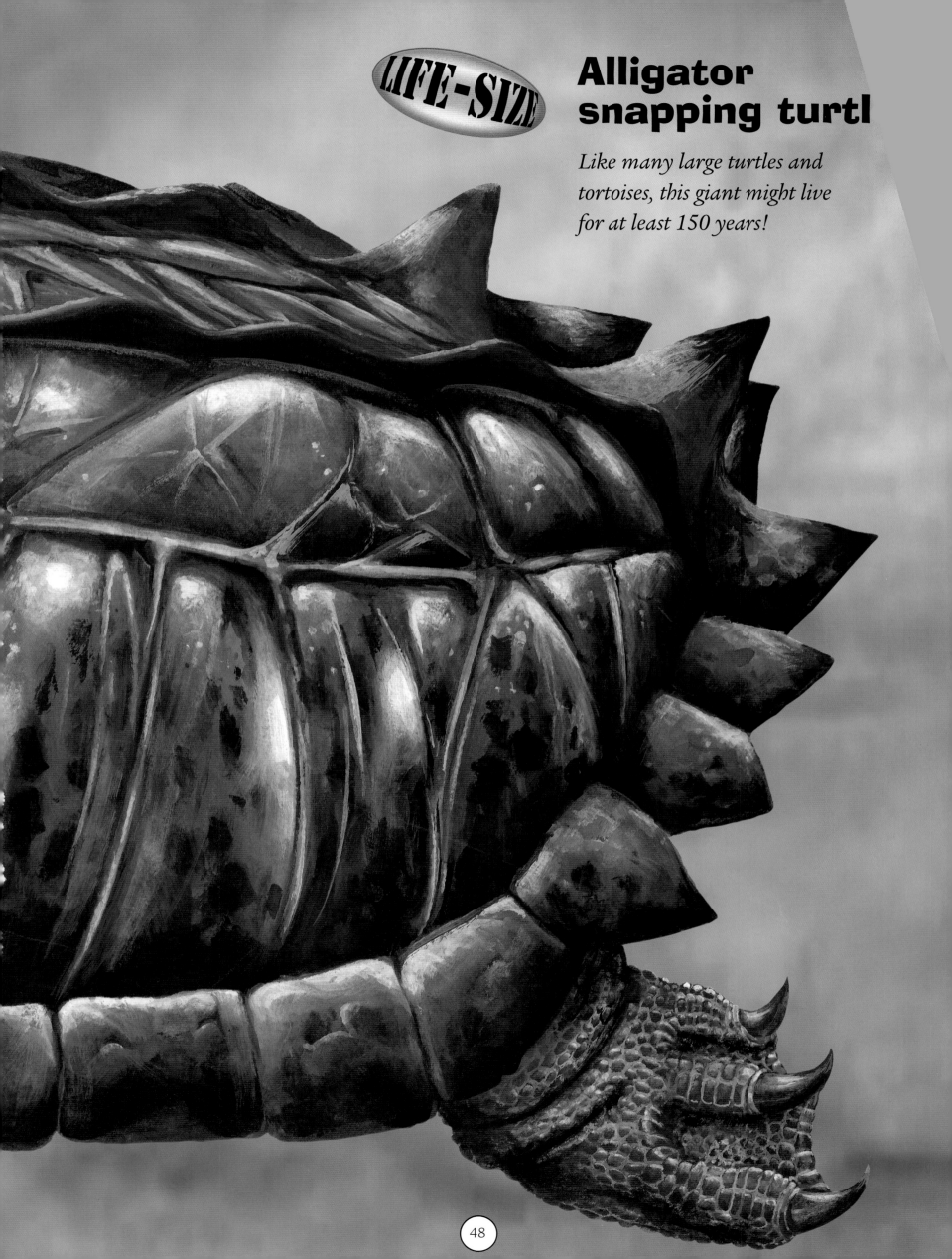

Alligator snapping turtl

Like many large turtles and tortoises, this giant might live for at least 150 years!

INDEX

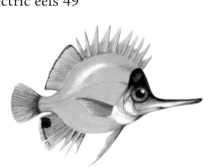

LIFE-SIZE KILLER CREATURES

WRITTEN BY

DANIEL GILPIN

Contents

Killing to eat

The great majority of killer creatures are predators that hunt and kill for food. Predators have special adaptations to help them kill other animals. Some have claws for grabbing prey and most have sharp teeth. The sperm whale is the largest predator on Earth – in fact, it is the world's fifth biggest animal. Adult males can reach 60 feet (18 m) long and weigh up to 55 tons (50 metric tons). The sperm whale breathes air, but it can hold its breath underwater for over two hours. Often, sperm whales dive to great depths to find their prey. This one is attacking a giant squid. Sperm whales have been detected over 1 mile (2 km) below the surface.

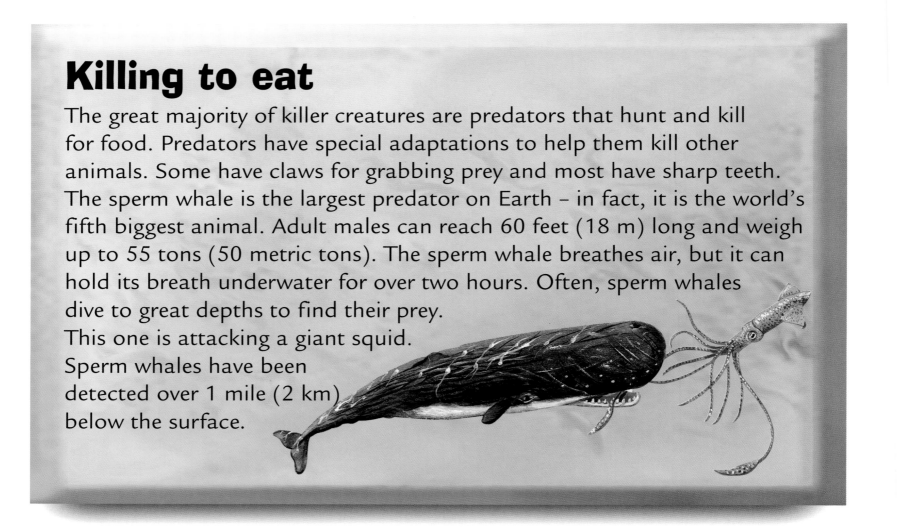

Crushed underfoot

Although it is a plant-eater, the common hippopotamus is Africa's most dangerous mammal. Every year, hippos kill more people than lions, hyenas or leopards. Hippos are dangerous because of their size. By day, they spend most of their time in the water, where they sometimes overturn boats and injure people with their massive teeth.

But it is at night, when hippos come onto land to feed, that they are most dangerous. Anyone who accidentally walks between a hippo and the water risks being trampled to death. Despite their size, hippos are fast runners and charge at anything that blocks their way.

Hippo's foot

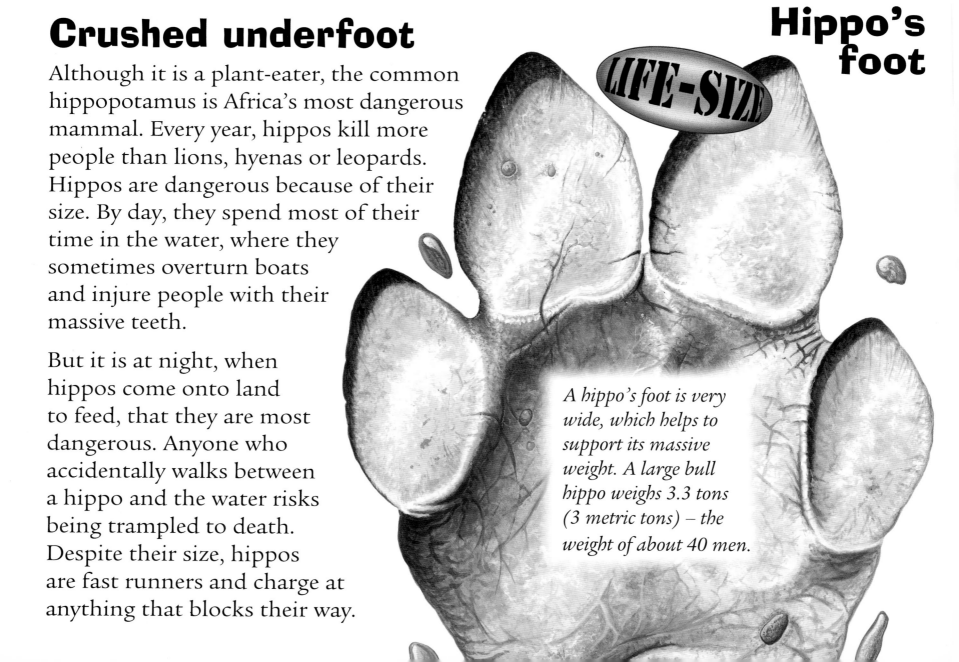

LIFE-SIZE

A hippo's foot is very wide, which helps to support its massive weight. A large bull hippo weighs 3.3 tons (3 metric tons) – the weight of about 40 men.

... and why do they do it?

Animals kill for a number of reasons. Many have to kill in order to eat. Some kill to defend themselves or their young. A few animals kill others by spreading disease and sometimes male animals kill their rivals when fighting for mates.

Deadly cargo

Some of the most deadly creatures look harmless. Few people would expect to be killed by a rat and even fewer by a flea. Yet these two creatures caused the deaths of a third of the population of Europe in the 14th century – about 34 million people! Together they spread bubonic plague, also known as the Black Death. The fleas carried the disease and lived on the bodies of rats.

When an infected rat flea bit someone, that person became ill with the plague and generally died. Bubonic plague can now be treated, and there are still a few cases around today. For example, chipmunks and other rodents give plague to about 15 people in the United States every year.

Life-size stamp

This stamp shows which killer creatures are illustrated as life-size in this book. It's just as surprising to see how tiny some things are, as to see how big they are. It's not possible to show all the creatures life-size – the sperm whale and giant squid on the right are so big that they would need pages as wide as two double-decker buses to appear at full size! When creatures are not shown life-size, a human footprint is often included to give a sense of scale.

x 10

Rat flea

Black rat

Fleas live by sucking the blood of larger creatures. Rat fleas live among the fur of rats and only bite humans when they are infected with the plague bug.

WHAT IS A KILLER?

A killer creature is an animal that kills other animals or humans. Most killer creatures are predators, which hunt and kill for food, but some cause death by spreading disease.

Food pyramid

Killer creatures are just one part of the natural world. They could not survive without something to kill. The way living things interact with each other can be shown as a pyramid. Plants form the base of the pyramid. Without them no animal could survive. There are more plants than all the animals put together. Plant-eaters survive by feeding only on plants and they form the next layer of the pyramid. A few killer creatures may eat fruits or other plant food, but their diet always includes the meat of other animals. The largest killers are found at the top of the pyramid. They are the "top predators" because nothing hunts these mighty killers.

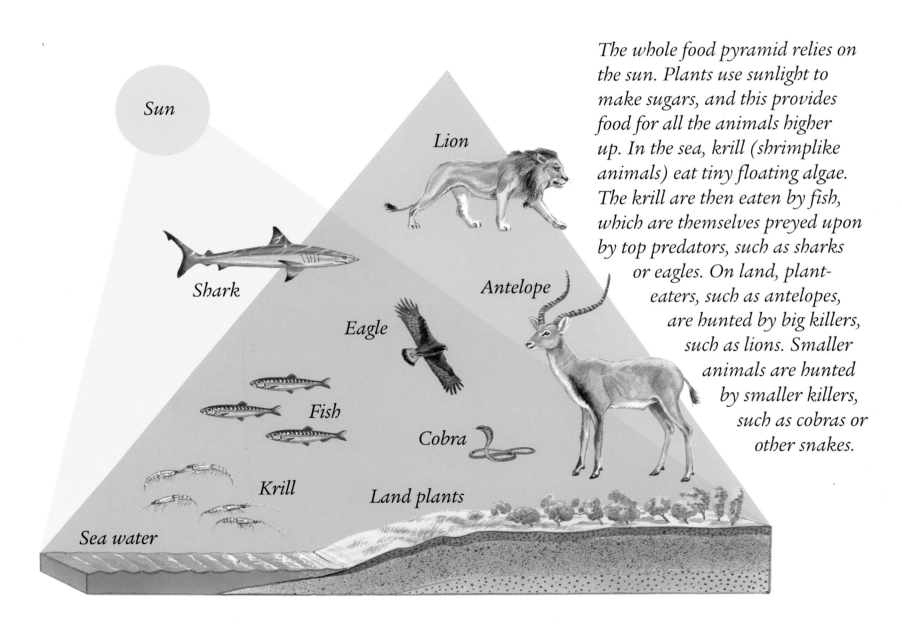

The whole food pyramid relies on the sun. Plants use sunlight to make sugars, and this provides food for all the animals higher up. In the sea, krill (shrimplike animals) eat tiny floating algae. The krill are then eaten by fish, which are themselves preyed upon by top predators, such as sharks or eagles. On land, plant-eaters, such as antelopes, are hunted by big killers, such as lions. Smaller animals are hunted by smaller killers, such as cobras or other snakes.

Sun

Lion

Shark

Antelope

Eagle

Fish

Cobra

Krill

Land plants

Sea water

Power struggles

Many male animals fight fiercely for mates. In some species, one male mates with many females after fighting off rivals. A dominant male has to work hard to keep his position. Eventually, he is bound to be defeated by a younger and stronger challenger. If he is unlucky, he may even be killed.

Some male animals show off their weapons as a warning to rivals and so avoid unnecessary fights. The male mandrill has a brightly colored face and long canine teeth that stick out of his mouth to scare away less powerful males.

Mandrill

The mandrill is the world's biggest monkey, growing to the size of a large dog. It lives on the floor of the tropical rain forests of Africa. It feeds mainly on fruits. A single male mandrill rules a troop of about 20 monkeys. The leader spends a lot of his time scaring off other males with a fierce snarl.

HOW CREATURES KILL

Predators have different weapons for killing their prey. Some have powerful jaws and sharp teeth, and kill with a crushing bite. Others inject their victims with venom or kill by using electric shocks.

Shock tactics

A few fish use electricity to stun and kill prey. The most famous of these is the electric eel, which lives in the rivers and swamps of South America. The electric eel generates electricity using its muscles, giving its tail a positive charge and its head a negative one. The eel locates prey by picking up the tiny electric fields produced by the bodies of other fish. Then the eel stuns its victims with a huge electric shock.

Another type of electric fish lives in the ocean. Called the torpedo ray, it too kills prey using electric shocks. Rather than using its whole body, the torpedo ray builds up an electric charge in special muscles called electric organs, which are located behind its head.

Electric eels keep growing throughout their life. The largest may reach 9 feet (2.7 m) long, but even young eels like this one can generate charges of 650 volts – more than twice as much as a wall socket generates.

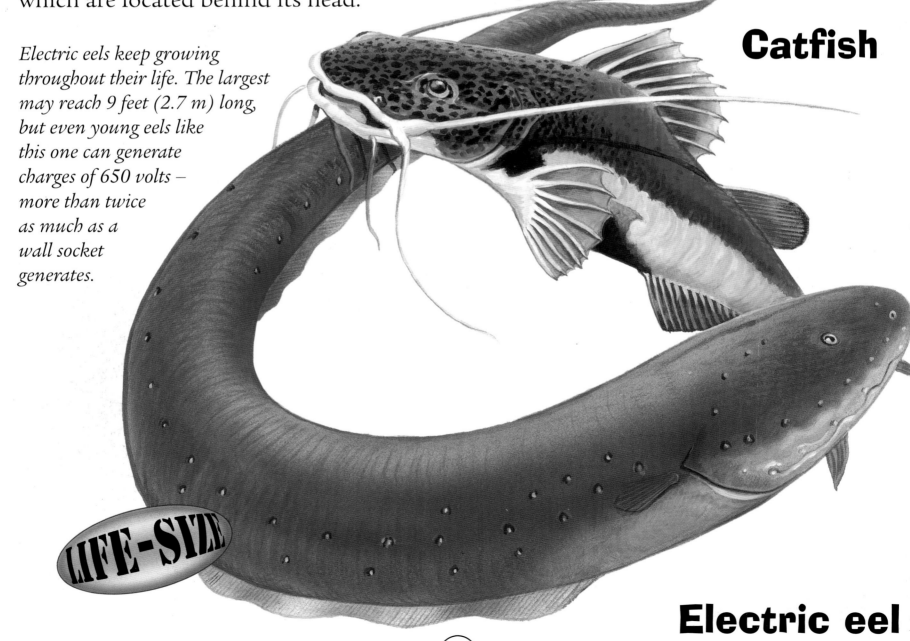

Catfish

LIFE-SIZE

Electric eel

Terrible teeth

The main weapon most predators have to kill prey is their teeth. A predator's teeth are designed to cut and stab into flesh like knives. Those that stab are used for gripping and usually point backward to help hold on to prey.

Killer mammals have several kinds of teeth. The stabbing fangs are known as canines and tend to be longer than the other kinds of teeth in the mouth. Cutting teeth have sharp edges for slicing off chunks of meat. In mammals such as the lion and coyote, the cheek teeth are known as carnassials. They form rows behind the canines. The carnassials in the upper and lower jaws move past each other like the blades of scissors.

Some predators, such as the great white shark, have teeth that both stab and cut. Sharks' teeth have serrated edges like the blade of a steak knife, which make them even better at slicing through prey.

Lion

Coyote

Tasmanian devil

Lions, coyotes and Tasmanian devils have canine teeth that suit the sizes of their prey. These hunters generally kill with a powerful bite.

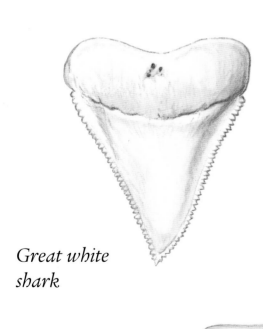

All 28 of a sperm whale's teeth form giant points. A great white shark uses about 3,000 teeth in its life. When one falls out, a new tooth is pushed up to take its place.

Great white shark

Sperm whale

LOCATING PREY

For predators, catching and killing victims is only half the battle. They have to find their prey first. Many predators have super-sharp senses to help them search and pick up sights, sounds, or smells other animals would miss.

LIFE-SIZE

Python

Heat seeker

Some snakes have an extra sense few other creatures possess. They can detect the heat produced by their victim's bodies. This special sense lets them hunt in complete darkness and capture prey that cannot see them coming. Rattlesnakes, boas and pythons have pits on their faces that pick up this body heat. The snakes use the pits alongside other senses to pinpoint prey before striking.

All land-living snakes have another incredible sense – they taste the air. Their forked tongues pick up particles emitted by prey, which are analyzed by an organ in the mouth.

A reticulated python's forked tongue is so sensitive it can detect where a victim is. If more tell-tale particles from prey are picked up by the left half of the fork than the right, then the snake turns left. The python's heat-seeking pits are small hollows on the snout.

All ears

The slightest rustle is all a serval needs to find its food. This African cat hunts mice and other rodents in the long grass of the savannah, where sight and smell are not enough to find prey. The serval's hearing is improved by its huge ears, which swivel like radar dishes in the direction of the tiniest noise. Once it has picked up a sound, the long-legged cat bounds toward it and pounces, sometimes not even seeing its prey until it is under its paws.

The serval listens for its prey in long grass. Its tall outer ears collect lots of sound waves and direct them all into the cat's inner ear. This allows the serval to pick up very faint noises.

Serval

LIFE-SIZE

Paws and claws

Lions and other cats kill their prey with a powerful bite that snaps the neck or clamps the windpipe shut so the victim cannot breathe. However, lions also have fearsome claws, which they use as grappling hooks to hold on to their struggling victims.

Most cats keep their claws sharp by retracting them when they are not in use. Each claw is pulled back into its sheath by elastic skin so that it does not get worn down or broken as the animal runs along. When the claws are needed for attack, the tiny muscles draw them out of their sheaths ready for action. As well as helping grip prey, the claws rip skin and flesh, making the prey weak and exhausted and easier to kill.

Lion's paw

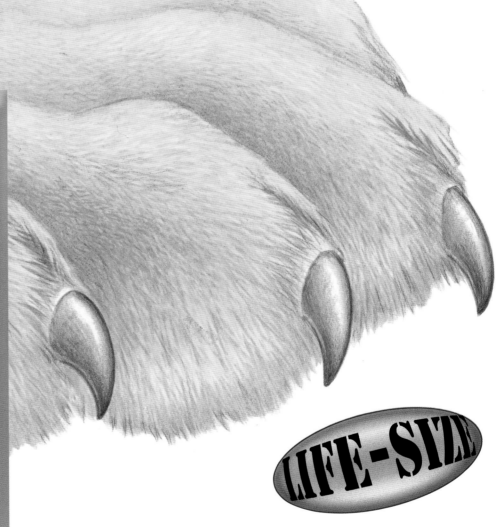

LIFE-SIZE

A lion's paw has soft, leathery pads for grip and huge, razor-sharp claws. The claws are held within the paw when the lion is moving to keep them sharp, but are flicked out like switchblades during an attack.

Weird ways of killing

Some creatures kill in very unusual ways. Mantis shrimps, for instance, punch their prey to death. The power of their flicking forelimbs is so great that they can even smash their way out of fish tanks. Bolas spiders lasso moths by swinging a blob of sticky silk. Cone snails harpoon their prey with their pointed tongues, while ant-lion larvae trap ants in sandy pits. The ants cannot climb out once they fall in and are paralyzed by the ant lion's venom.

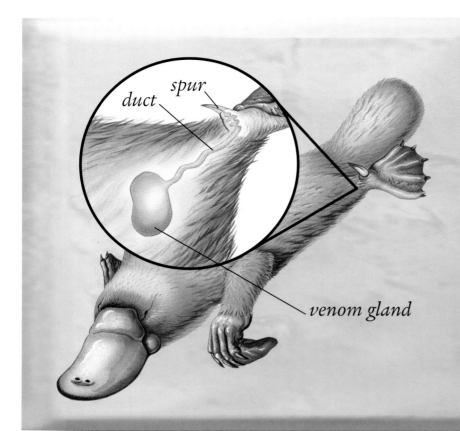

Toxic stab

The male duck-billed platypus has venomous spurs on its hind legs. The spurs are used mainly to attack rivals, but if attacked a platypus will use them to defend itself. In the days when platypuses were shot for their fur, dogs were sometimes poisoned trying to pull wounded platypuses from the water. The venom is made in a gland inside the leg and travels to the spur through a duct, or tube.

spur

duct

venom gland

Lethal injection

While the teeth of many predators are used for gripping and cutting up prey, some snakes have teeth that are used for injecting venom. These long, pointed teeth are known as fangs. They work like a syringe needle, pumping the poisons directly into victims' flesh. The venom is produced by glands in the snake's head and forced down through the hollow fangs as they bite into the prey. When not in use, the fangs of most venomous snakes are held flat against the roof of the mouth. They are flicked forward only at the moment of attack.

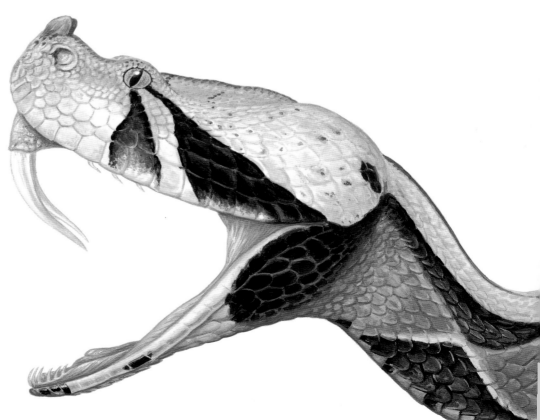

The gaboon viper has the longest fangs of any snake, reaching 2 inches (5 cm) from base to tip. This African reptile lies in wait for prey, perfectly camouflaged among the fallen leaves on the forest floor.

Gaboon viper

Following its nose

Many predatory mammals have a keen sense of smell. Dogs in particular use scent to find prey. Wolves, just like pet dogs, often follow their noses as they travel, sniffing around to pick up telltale odors and trails. Their long snouts are lined with a finely tuned smell-sensitive layer, which can detect even the faintest smells.

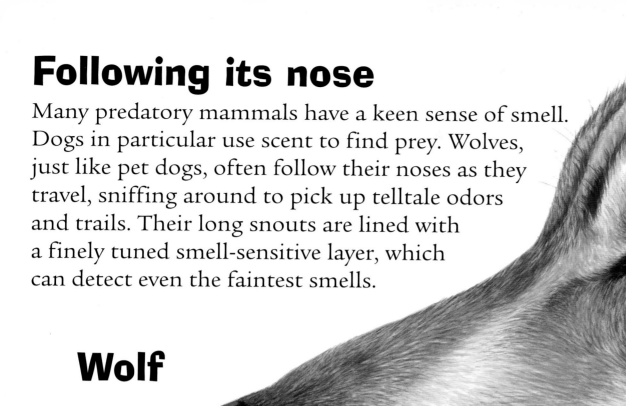

Wolf

By using its nose, a wolf can follow the trail of prey that is a long way off. Packs of wolves chase prey over huge distances and catch their victim once it is exhausted.

LIFE-SIZE

Hawk-eyed hunter

Like all birds of prey, the northern goshawk has excellent vision. It hunts by day, catching birds in flight and plucking squirrels from the branches of forest trees. The hawk's eyes can see four times more detail than our own.

Even the most agile birds have trouble getting away from a goshawk. Both the hawk's eyes point forward, not to the side. This allows the hawk to judge distances very accurately so it can attack fleeing prey with great precision.

The piercing eyes of the northern goshawk make it a deadly daylight hunter. The hawk kills prey with a claw, or talon, and rips off chunks of flesh with its hooked beak.

Goshawk

LIFE-SIZE

Killer whale

Top predator

As an ocean predator, the killer whale has no equal. It preys on other whales and even great white sharks. Male killer whales are 30 feet (9 m) long and weigh up to 11 tons (10 metric tons). Females are smaller but can still grow to more than 20 feet (6 m). Killer whales live and hunt in close-knit family groups called pods. Often the pod works together to catch and kill prey and it can overpower any sea creature. Even the world's largest animal, the blue whale, has been known to fall victim to killer-whale attacks.

OCEAN KILLERS

The sea has more killer creatures than anywhere else.
Some are small and kill their prey using venom,
but others are true monsters that strike their victims
with overpowering force.

Killer bite

The ocean killers most feared by people are sharks.
These large, fast-moving fish attack suddenly and with
frightening power, tearing chunks off prey with their
vicious, razor-sharp teeth.

The most feared shark of all is the biggest hunting fish,
the great white. It hunts seals and other large prey along
coasts, surging up from below to smash into its victims
with jaws wide open. Prey dies quickly as it loses blood
from the shark's enormous bites. Then the shark
returns to feed. Great whites, along with several
other shark species, sometimes kill humans.

*The great white shark is a massive predator that strikes without
warning. Big individuals may be 23 feet (7 m) long and weigh over
3.3 tons (3 metric tons), yet they can move with incredible speed.*

Soft touch

The box jellyfish is one of the most deadly sea creatures of all. Every year, it attacks dozens of people with a powerful venom injected by millions of stinging cells. These release tiny poisonous darts when they make contact with something. The slightest touch of the box jellyfish's soft tentacles can mean death. Many swimmers are stung when these killers swarm off the coasts of Australia. One person dies from their stings every two years.

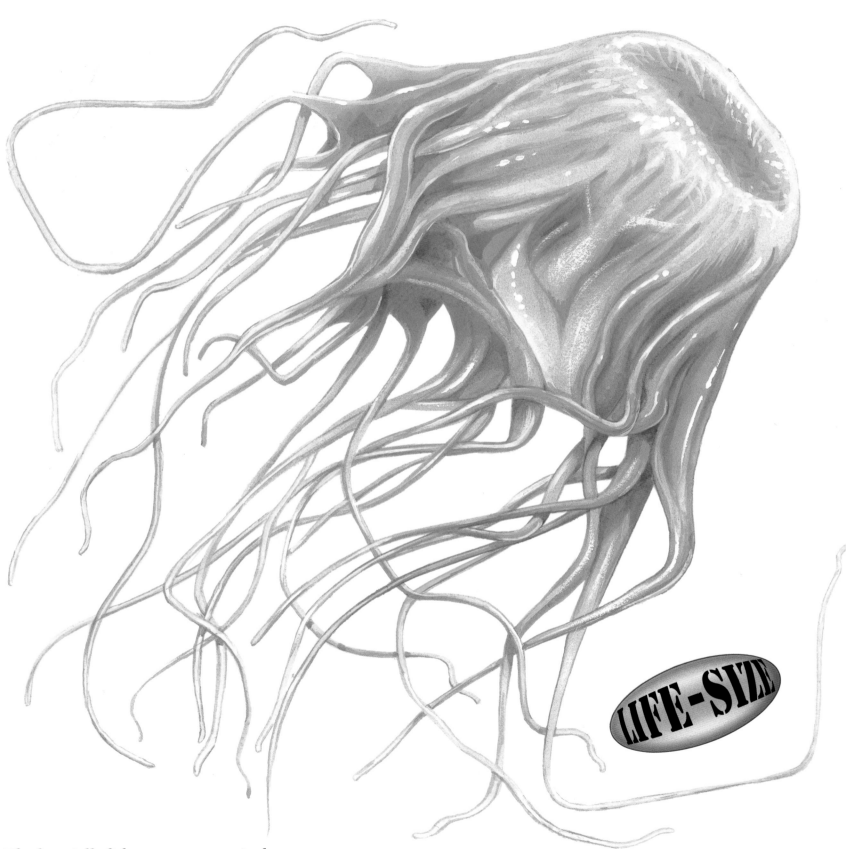

The box jellyfish, or sea wasp, is the most venomous animal in the sea. Left untreated, its stings can cause death by heart failure in as little as three minutes.

Box jellyfish

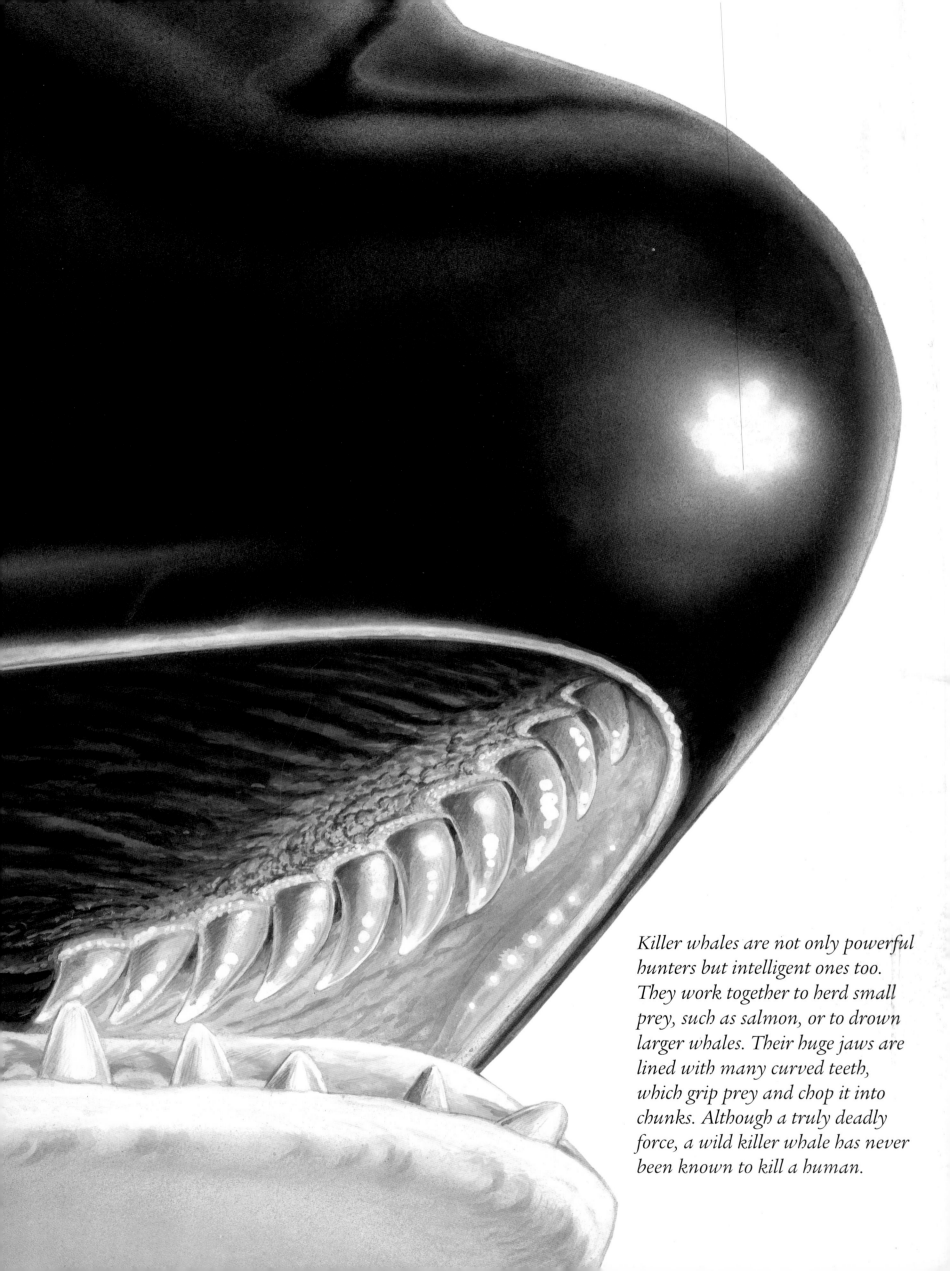

Killer whales are not only powerful
hunters but intelligent ones too.
They work together to herd small
prey, such as salmon, or to drown
larger whales. Their huge jaws are
lined with many curved teeth,
which grip prey and chop it into
chunks. Although a truly deadly
force, a wild killer whale has never
been known to kill a human.

ICE AND SNOW

The world's polar regions have their own killer creatures. In the Antarctic, the leopard seal hunts penguins and other swimming prey. At the other end of Earth, the polar bear rules the Arctic.

White death

The polar bear is one of the largest land-living predators on Earth. It is much more carnivorous than most bears and roams the sea ice for meat. The polar bear hunts mainly by smell, following the scent of seals and seabirds that are resting on the ice. It also lies in wait for prey, lurking around the holes in the ice that seals use when they come up to breathe.

Although the polar bear is the top predator in the Arctic, it is not the only killer. Wolves hunt here for land-based prey, such as reindeer and musk oxen. Smaller creatures are hunted by the Arctic fox, which also follows polar bears to feed on their leftovers.

The polar bear uses its huge paws to club its prey and pin it down on the ice. The paws are broad and flat to spread the polar bear's weight, and have small webs between the toes to make them more effective paddles for swimming.

Polar bear's paw

Chiller killer

The leopard seal is one of the most deadly creatures in the waters of the Southern Ocean around Antarctica. These giant killers can be more than 10 feet (3 m) long. They patrol along the edge of the ice pack looking for their chief prey – penguins diving for food. Leopard seals kill with a bite from their massive jaws, which are lined with long teeth. They will even prey on smaller types of seal.

Clash of the titans

The walrus is a formidable creature armed with massive, downward-pointing tusks. Males use these tusks when sparring for dominance, and the tusks are also used as defensive weapons against polar bears. Massive walruses can even kill attacking polar bears by stabbing them to death. As a result, polar bears approach only young or old walruses and only when they are extremely hungry. Although they look fearsome, walruses feed mainly on shellfish. They squirt jets of water from their mouths to uncover food buried in the sand on the bottom of the seabed.

Male walruses use their long tusks in battles over mates. Females also have tusks, although they tend to be smaller. Walruses live on the ice pack around the North Pole. Fully grown adults weigh more than a ton.

MOUNTAINS AND FOREST

The cold northern forests and high places of the world have their own unique predators. Some prowl or clamber in search of prey, while others soar high overhead.

Adaptable hunter

The puma hunts in many habitats and is known by many names. In North America, it is often called the cougar or mountain lion. The puma is a stealthy predator that silently stalks its prey, picking its way with ease through the rocks of the mountains and slipping silently through the forest. It has excellent vision and hunts mainly by day, often spotting its victims from a long way off. The puma is the most widespread cat in the world, inhabiting a variety of climates from Canada in the north all the way down to southern Chile and Argentina.

The puma is at home in both mountains and forest. Like most cats, it is a solitary hunter, spending the majority of its life on its own.

High flier

The Andean condor has the biggest wings of any bird. Spanning over 10 feet (3 m) from tip to tip, the wings are also very broad to catch rising columns of warm air, called thermals. Condors ride the thermals to the peaks of the Andes Mountains in South America, where they live. The Andean condor lives mainly by scavenging, soaring over mountainsides and valleys in search of dead animals such as llamas and deer. The condors also glide down to the Pacific coast and feast on the bodies of dead seals and whales that have washed up on the shore.

A condor swoops onto the body of a viscacha – a large rodent. The giant bird will also kill weak and injured animals using its huge talons and hooked beak.

Tough customer

The wolverine is the largest member of the weasel family, growing to about the size of a Labrador dog. It lives in the mountains and forests of Scandinavia, Siberia, and North America. Wolverines hunt a wide range of prey, including many animals that are larger than themselves. It has a voracious appetite, which has earned it another name – "the glutton."

For its size, the wolverine is an extremely powerful and violent animal. It has been known to attack deer as large as moose by jumping on them from trees and biting their necks.

The wolverine has a long, shaggy coat to keep it warm in the cold places it inhabits. Its wide feet act like snowshoes and allow it to run over soft snow. Many of the wolverine's victims sink into the snow, making them easy targets.

Wolverine

NIGHTTIME ATTACK

Many killer creatures hunt at night, pouncing on their victims in the darkness. Most have heightened senses to help them find their prey and must move silently to avoid waking or startling their victims.

Glow in the dark

Leopards catch prey by stealth. They creep up on victims silently, then charge in suddenly to grab them before they can escape. In the forest, leopards sometimes hunt by day. The spotted coat acts as camouflage in the dappled shade. More often though, the cat seeks out prey at night, using the cover of darkness to hide itself completely. The leopard, like all cats, has excellent vision. A mirrored surface at the backs of its eyes helps the eye gather more light, so the cat can see six times better than we can by the light of the moon or the stars.

LIFE-SIZE

Leopard

A leopard's eyes are so good at collecting light that it has to protect them by day. In bright sunlight, the pupils become very small to restrict the amount of light coming in. At night, they widen to let in as much light as possible.

Water vacuum

The hellbender is a giant salamander that lives in the rivers and streams of North America. It is the world's third largest amphibian, growing to about 28 inches (70 cm) long. The largest amphibian, the Chinese giant salamander reaches 5.9 feet (1.8 m). Hellbenders hunt at night, gulping down crawfish and fish by drawing them into the mouth with a powerful suck.

False vampire bat

Keeping an ear out

The spectral vampire is the world's largest meat-eating bat. Like most hunting bats, it can find its prey using echolocation, emitting high-pitched squeaks and then listening for the echoes that bounce back. However, the spectral vampire bat of South America also uses its excellent hearing to listen out for prey. It hunts for roosting birds, fish and even other bats.

Spectral vampires do not drink blood like other vampire bats. These smaller bats use their razor-sharp teeth to cut out small pieces of flesh then lap up the warm blood with their tongues.

LIFE-SIZE

The false vampire bat is only a few inches long but has a wingspan of almost 3.3 feet (1 m). Once it hears a victim moving, the bat swoops on it suddenly, killing it with a crushing bite from its powerful jaws.

Crushing coils

The rivers and swamps of South America are home to the world's heaviest snake – the green anaconda. This huge serpent can weigh as much as three adult men and grow to 28 feet (8.5 m) long. Although it occasionally comes out onto land, the anaconda spends most of its time in the water, which helps to support its bulky body. The anaconda hunts capybaras (giant relatives of guinea pigs), peccaries (relatives of wild pigs), and even other hunters such as crocodiles. The snake wraps its coils around a victim and slowly tightens its grip until the prey stops breathing.

Like all snakes, anacondas cannot chew or bite off chunks of flesh. Instead they must swallow prey whole. Anacondas eat prey with bodies much wider than their own heads, so they must detach their jawbones to swallow their meals.

RIVERS AND SWAMPS

Water can be a great place to hide. Many killer creatures lurk beneath it, waiting to attack animals that come down to drink. More predators hunt animals that live in the water, while others kill on land but return to swamps, lakes, or rivers to breed.

Tropical monster

The goliath frog does most of its hunting in water, feeding mainly on insect larvae, crustaceans, and small fish. However, the frog does sometimes eat lizards and small mammals living on the riverbank. It inhabits fast-flowing streams and rivers in West Africa. But as the world's largest frog, this species has become very rare because many are taken from the wild as pets.

The goliath frog weighs more than 8 pounds (3.5 kg), the same weight as a newborn baby. The frog's body is about 12 inches (30 cm) long. It can jump 10 feet (3 m) in one bound.

Goliath frog

LIFE-SIZE

Surprise attack

The saltwater crocodile is the world's biggest reptile, growing to 23 feet (7 m) long and weighing more than a ton. This monstrous predator lives in mangrove swamps and river estuaries around Southeast Asia and Australia. It includes human beings among its prey. As its name suggests, the crocodile often enters the sea and sometimes swims out to remote islands.

A close relative of the saltwater crocodile, the Nile crocodile is almost as big and also kills humans. Every year, about 1,000 people meet their death in its jaws, making it one of Africa's most deadly creatures.

This saltwater crocodile is attacking a water buffalo. Crocodiles kill prey by pulling it underwater. They roll over and over until their victim has drowned.

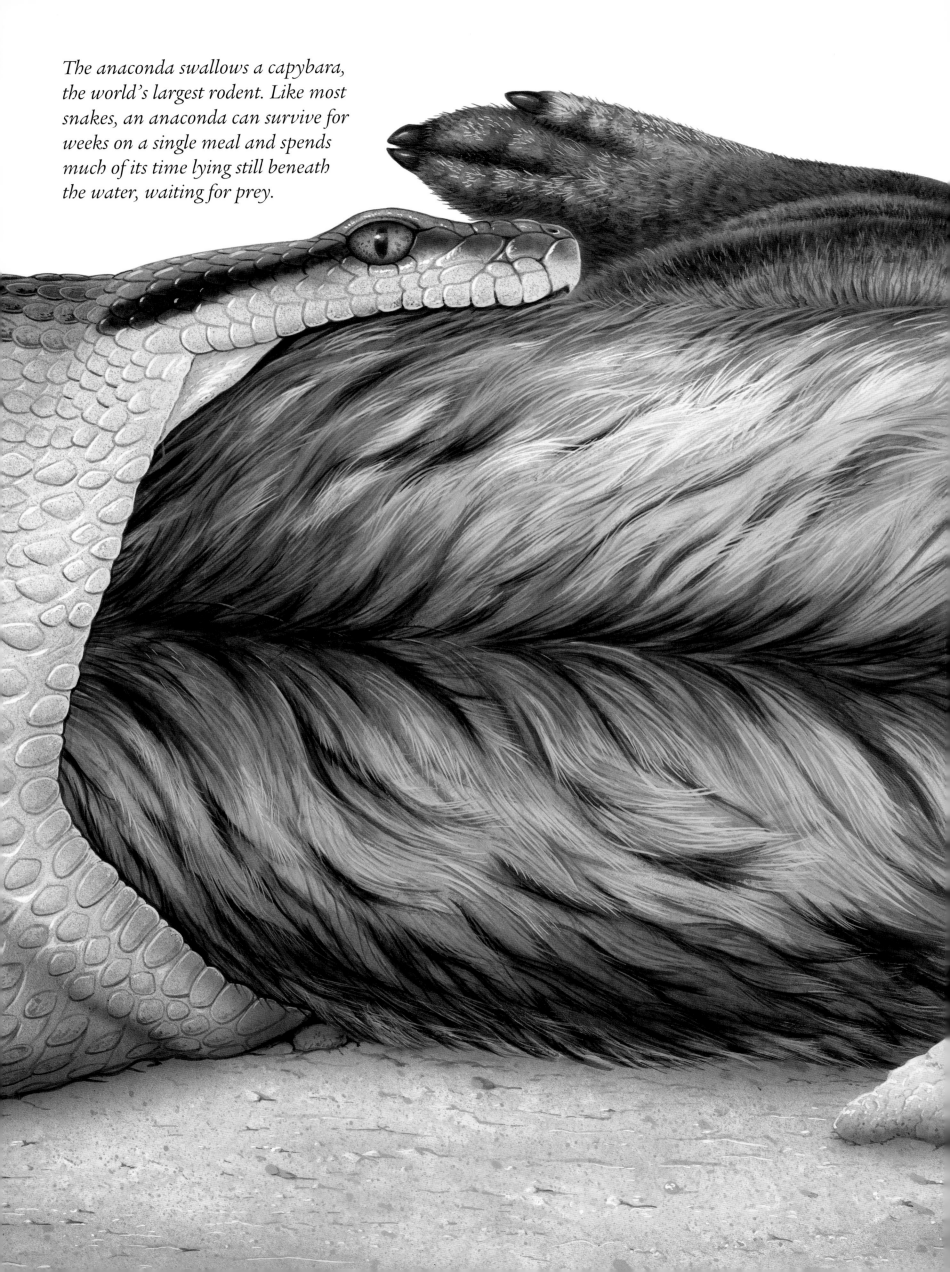

The anaconda swallows a capybara, the world's largest rodent. Like most snakes, an anaconda can survive for weeks on a single meal and spends much of its time lying still beneath the water, waiting for prey.

Green anaconda

LIFE-SIZE

GRASSLAND

The world's grasslands are a battleground between hunters and the hunted. With little cover to hide them, most animals here rely on speed or teamwork to survive. Grasslands are home to the fastest land animals on Earth, as well as some of the largest and most powerful pack-hunting predators.

Sting in the tail

Scorpions are common predators of both grasslands and deserts. They are related to spiders and all of them are killers. Scorpions are armed with fearsome pincers, which they use to catch most of their prey. Larger victims are paralyzed with a stab from the tail, which injects them with a dose of venom. Scorpions also use their venomous tails for defense, stinging any animal foolhardy enough to come too close.

The imperial scorpion, from West Africa, is one of the largest in the world. It can deliver a painful sting and it is best to leave them alone. However, some animals, such as baboons, catch them to eat.

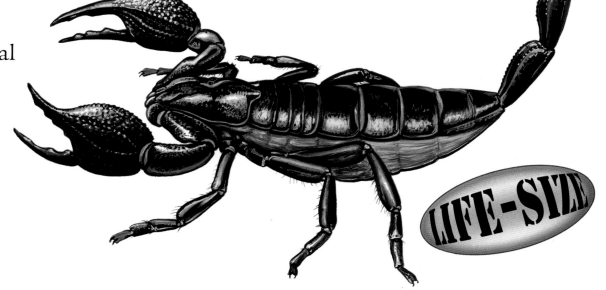

LIFE-SIZE

Imperial scorpion

Bad to the bone

The spotted hyena is one of the most feared animals on the African grassland. Although it has a reputation for scavenging, it is also an accomplished hunter. Spotted hyenas live in large families called clans. The clans can chase down and kill almost any prey. As scavengers, they will wait for leftovers but steal food from other predators. Large clans can even frighten off prides of lions.

The spotted hyena has large teeth and extremely powerful jaws. These are used both for killing and for dismembering prey, crushing bones into splinters to get at the tasty marrow inside.

LIFE-SIZE

Spotted hyena

Sprint finisher

The cheetah is the world's fastest land-living animal, capable of running at speeds of at least 60 miles (96 km) per hour. It has to be quick, as the gazelles it hunts are also very fleet of foot. Unlike other cats, the cheetah does not sheath its claws while running. It has them stuck out all the time like running spikes to give its paws extra grip.

The cheetah must judge the moment to pounce to the second. If it gets it wrong, the cat might get a nasty wound from being stabbed by the sharp horns many of its prey use for protection.

The cheetah is not only fast but has explosive acceleration. It can run from 0 to 60 miles (0–100 km) per hour in less than 3 seconds. That is faster than any sports car on the road!

Silent giant

In Asia, the tiger is ruler of the jungle, the most powerful killer that rules unopposed. Despite its size, a tiger stalks its prey unseen, camouflaged by its stripes in the broken shade of the undergrowth. The tiger is the largest cat of all, slightly larger than the lion. Unlike lions, which live in prides, tigers hunt alone. When they get close enough to a victim, such as a wild pig or deer, the tiger rushes out from its hiding place and knocks the prey off its feet. Then the giant cat can deliver a fatal bite to the neck.

IN THE JUNGLE

The tropical forests are home to more species of animal than any other habitat. Predators here exist in mind-boggling numbers and come in a huge range of shapes and sizes.

Fangs for everything

With a leg-span big enough to cover a dinner plate, the Goliath bird-eating spider is the largest spider in the world. This eight-legged monster lives in the rain forests of South America and spends the day in a burrow. As night falls, it emerges to hunt, scouring the forest floor and clambering up trees in search of prey. The bird-eating spider does live up to its name by killing small birds in their nests. However, frogs, lizards, and mice are more common victims. The spider kills with a downward stab of its two venomous fangs.

Goliath bird-eating spider

LIFE-SIZE

Like all spiders, the bird-eating spider cannot chew. Instead, it pumps digestive juices into its dying prey and sucks up the resulting fleshy goo.

Marching into battle

The world's largest centipedes live in jungles, with a few species reaching 12 inches (30 cm) long. These predators are large compared to other creepy-crawlies. They kill prey on the forest floor with a stab from poisonous claws beside their mouths.

Most of the centipede's victims are insects, but they also eat mice and other small mammals. The word *centipede* means "one hundred feet," but most have less than this. Nevertheless, they have more legs than any other killer creature.

Weapon of war

Many people think of chimpanzees as cute animals, but they can be extremely violent. Male chimps often gang up to attack a rival and sometimes beat them to death.

Chimpanzees are also aggressive hunters, working together to chase monkeys through the trees. The chimps tear victims to pieces using their strong arms and sharp teeth. Besides using brute strength, chimps also use their intelligence to kill. They throw sticks and stones to scare adult forest pigs away from their young. The apes then kill the piglets left behind.

Chimps are among the few animals that use tools, and they often wield large sticks to frighten rivals.

LIFE-SIZE

Tiger centipede

Tiger centipedes live in the rain forests of South and Central America. The legs in the middle of the body are longer than those nearer each end. The longer ones can step over the legs in front, so the centipede does not get in a tangle as it scuttles along.

LIFE-SIZE

Tiger

The tiger is one of the world's biggest and most fearsome killer creatures, weighing twice as much as the average man. Some tigers have been known to develop a taste for human flesh, hunting people when they become too old or weak to catch their usual prey.

KILLERS OF THE PAST

Today's killer creatures include some fearsome animals, but even more terrifying predators lived in the past. We know of these creatures because their remains are preserved in rocks as fossils, which scientists can examine to determine how long ago they lived.

Feathered fiend

For millions of years, the terror birds were South America's top killers. These flightless giants stood 10 feet (3 m) tall and had huge hooked beaks as long as a horse's head. Although massive, the terror birds were fast movers, capable of chasing down prey at high speed. Terror birds lived until quite recently. They finally died out 15,000 years ago, not long before the first humans arrived in South America.

Terror birds have some smaller living relatives called the seriemas, which kill by smashing their victims against the ground. Terror birds may have killed this way as well.

KILLERS GREAT AND SMALL

When it comes to hunting, size is often important. Big animals are stronger and find it easier to kill prey. The world's greatest killers, however, are actually tiny. Can you guess what they are?

Mighty roar

The Kodiak bear is a type of giant grizzly that lives in Alaska. It is the world's biggest land predator. The Kodiak bear uses its enormous size as a weapon, both when fighting others of its own kind and when attacking large prey. However, Kodiak bears are not just voracious killers. They also eat a lot of fruit and other plant foods.

LIFE-SIZE

x 5

Only female mosquitoes bite, using long, pointed mouthparts like a sharp-ended straw. They seek out humans and other animals for a drink of blood, which they need to help their eggs develop.

Invisible killers

Diseases kill more people than wars, accidents and other killer creatures put together. Diseases are caused by microscopic organisms. Bacteria are tiny single cells. They cause diseases such as typhoid and cholera. Viruses are even smaller than bacteria. For example, the HIV virus is less than a millionth of a meter long. The HIV virus kills by attacking the body's defenses. Forty million people have HIV today. The most deadly creature is called Plasmodium. This protozoan causes malaria, the world's worst disease.

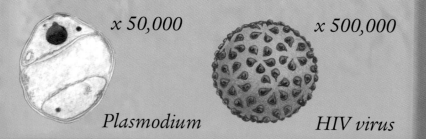

x 50,000   *x 500,000*

Plasmodium   *HIV virus*

Worst killer

The world's most deadly killer creature has no claws or pointed teeth, and when it attacks it is often barely noticed. It is the Anopheles mosquito, a tiny insect that lives in many warm parts of the world. The Anopheles mosquito kills by transmitting malaria, a disease that claims more than a million human lives every year. The disease is passed on in the mosquito's saliva when it bites and may take weeks or even months before it shows its first symptoms.

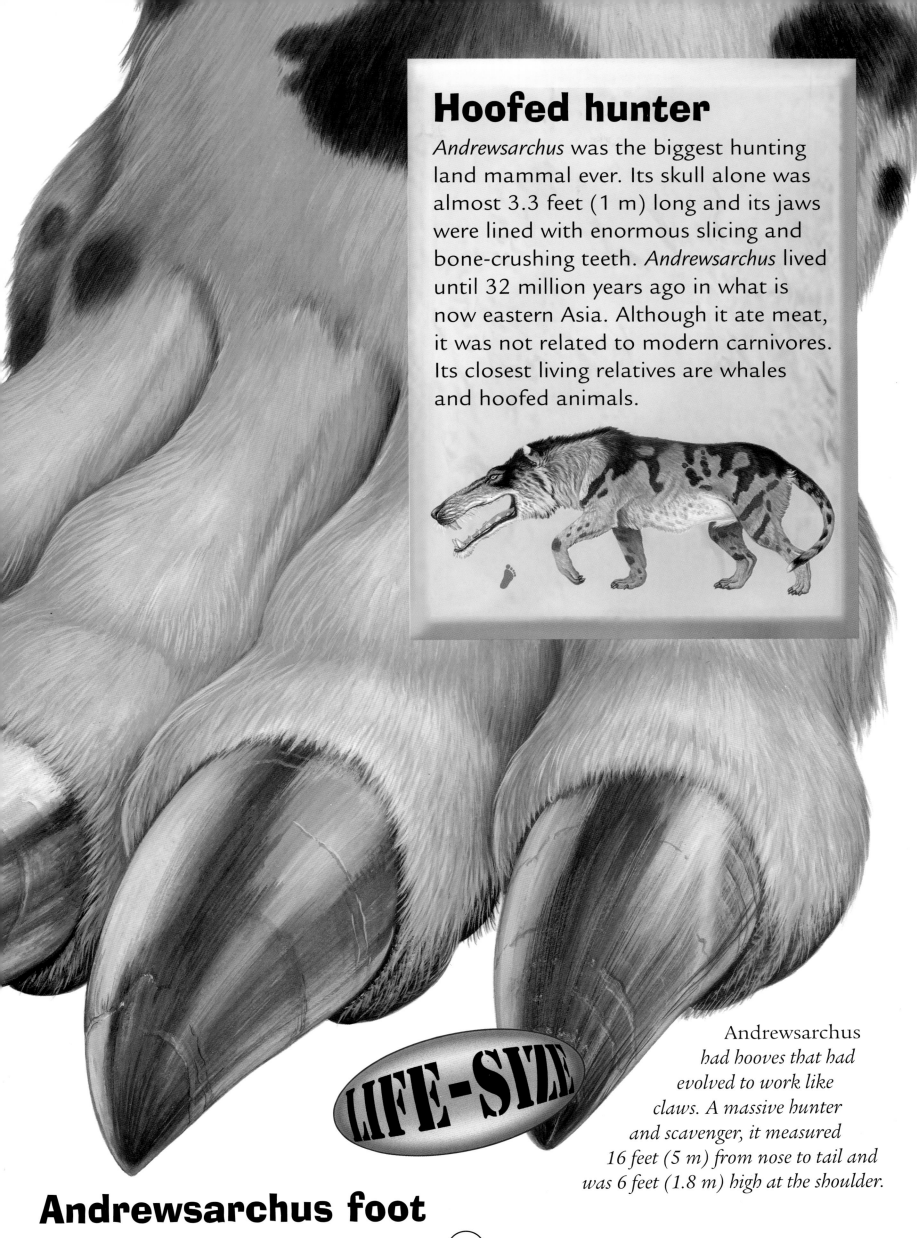

Hoofed hunter

Andrewsarchus was the biggest hunting land mammal ever. Its skull alone was almost 3.3 feet (1 m) long and its jaws were lined with enormous slicing and bone-crushing teeth. *Andrewsarchus* lived until 32 million years ago in what is now eastern Asia. Although it ate meat, it was not related to modern carnivores. Its closest living relatives are whales and hoofed animals.

LIFE-SIZE

Andrewsarchus *had hooves that had evolved to work like claws. A massive hunter and scavenger, it measured 16 feet (5 m) from nose to tail and was 6 feet (1.8 m) high at the shoulder.*

Andrewsarchus foot

LIFE-SIZE

Kodiak
bear

INDEX

LIFE-SIZE
REPTILES

WRITTEN BY
HANNAH WILSON

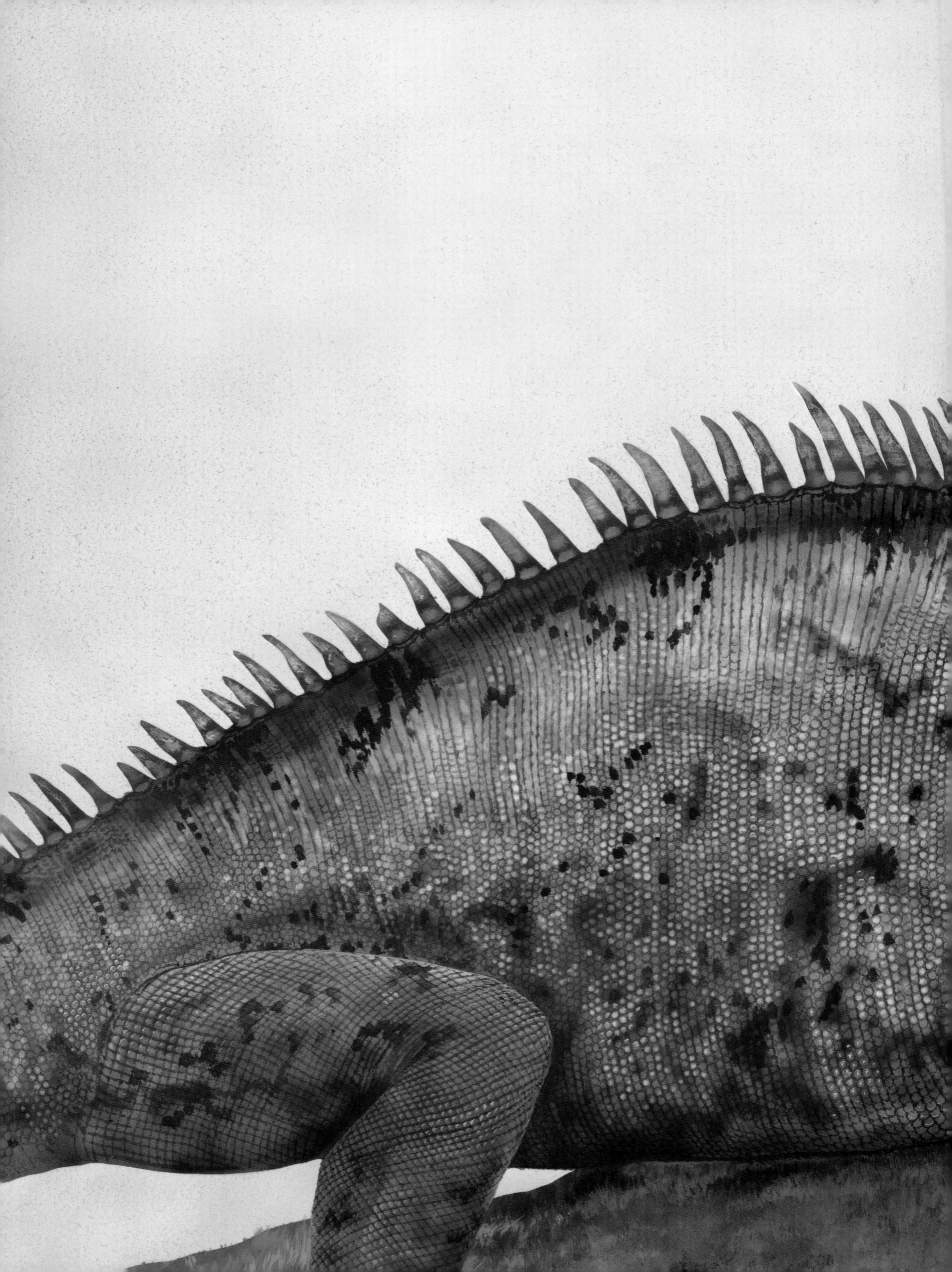

Contents

Staying alive

Most reptiles run away when they are under attack, but for lumbering tortoises that is not an option. Instead, they retreat into their armored shells. Other reptiles stay out of sight by being camouflaged. A chameleon can even change its color to match its surroundings! Other reptiles do not need to hide away. Coral snakes, for example, are brightly colored. This warns attackers that the snake's bite contains a deadly venom.

LIFE-SIZE

This skink is using a drastic defense tactic. The raccoon bites the bright blue tail of its prey instead of the head. The tail breaks off and continues to wriggle while the skink dashes to safety. The lizard soon grows a new tail.

Killing tactics

Most reptiles are hunters. Many kill a wide range of prey, but some are specialists. It's pretty clear what's on the menu for the ratsnake or the egg-eating snake. Reptiles catch their prey with their teeth, claws, or even a sticky tongue. Turtles slice up prey with sharp, beak-like jaws, while crocodiles drown antelopes by spinning them around underwater.

The reticulated python is a constrictor, it crushes its prey to death with its coils. This python is the world's longest snake, growing to 49 feet (15 meters), that's the length of a city bus!

Sensory skills

Reptiles have poor hearing. Some don't even have any ear openings at all. The forked tongues of snakes and some lizards are not very good at tasting either. Strangely, they are used for smelling instead. The tips of the tongue pick up scent particles in the air. The tips then slide into slots in the roof the mouth, so the reptile can detect the smells.

Reptiles have some other unusual sensory skills. Some snakes detect the heat given off by prey, using dips, or "pits", on their faces. And many lizards have a light-sensitive "third eye" inside the top of their skulls.

LIFE-SIZE

LIFE-SIZE

The long-nosed whipsnake has horizontal pupils so it can see to the front and to the side at the same time. To focus on its prey, it looks down grooves on its long snout, in the same way an archer looks along the length of an arrow to aim at a target.

The eyes of a chameleon can move independently and point in two different directions at the same time. This allows the lizard to scan its surroundings for food.

Eggs and babies

Most reptiles lay eggs, carefully hiding them in nests, but some snakes, such as rattlesnakes, and many lizards give birth to their young. Infant reptiles look like miniature adults, although their coloring is often different. Pythons are among the best reptile parents, a female will coil herself around the eggs. Her body keeps them warm until the young hatch.

LIFE-SIZE

A baby hawksbill turtle pushes its way out of its egg. Like bird eggs, reptile eggs have yolks, which nourish the young as they grow inside.

WHAT IS A REPTILE?

Scaly, spiky, horned, clawed or venomous, many reptiles are formidable creatures. Most belong to a group called the squamates, which includes lizards and snakes. Turtles and tortoises make up the second-largest group, while crocodiles and alligators account for less than one percent of all reptiles.

Reptiles long ago

Reptiles began to evolve about 340 million years ago from four-legged creatures that laid soft eggs in water. Reptilian eggs developed waterproof shells so they could be laid on dry land. The reptiles grew tough scaly skin and stronger skeletons as they adapted to a land-based life. And they grew larger. Much larger.

Some reptiles have changed little in millions of years. Proganochelys lived more than 200 million years ago but looked very much like a modern turtle.

Some prehistoric reptiles, like this pterosaur, could fly.

Many dinosaurs, like Plateosaurus, walked on their hind legs.

Saurosuchus, one of the first reptiles, was not a dinosaur but a relative of crocodiles.

About 200 million years ago, Earth was ruled by giant reptiles, dinosaurs. But the dinosaurs came to a dramatic end 65 million years ago when an asteroid (space rock) hit Earth. This produced an immense dust cloud that darkened the skies for years. Today's reptiles, like crocodiles and snakes, made it through the devastation. But the changes killed the dinosaurs. Only their descendants, birds, survive.

Sunbathing

Reptiles have no fur or feathers to keep them warm and cannot control their body temperature from the inside. Instead, they gain or lose heat from their surroundings, they are warmed by the sun or cooled by water. This is called "ectothermy". Many reptiles have to bask in the morning sun to warm up before beginning to hunt.

Life-size stamp

This stamp shows which reptiles are drawn life-size. It's not possible to show all the creatures life-size, the python on page 6 is as long as two flights of stairs! When a reptile is drawn on a smaller scale, the symbol of an adult human hand is sometimes shown to give a sense of how large the animal is.

powerful tail used for swimming

bony plates strengthen scales

Reptiles do not sweat through their tough skins, so alligators pant with their mouths open to cool down.

long claws

The body of this alligator is typical of many reptiles. It is low-lying, with short legs sticking out the side.

The teeth grow throughout the reptile's life.

Scaly skin

Reptilian scales are made of keratin, the same substance in your hair and fingernails. Scales make the skin waterproof. They can be thickened to form armored plates or shells. Scales do not grow, so a reptile sheds its skin when it becomes too small for it.

Snakes, such as this garter snake, can shed their skin all at once, but lizards shed skin in pieces because their legs get in the way.

LIZARDS

With more than 3,000 species, lizards can be as small as ladybugs or as large as alligators. Spotty, striped, smooth, or spiky, they live in deserts, jungles, and even the ocean. And some don't even have legs, if you see a slow worm in your garden, remember it's not a worm at all, nor a snake, it's a lizard!

Sticky fingers

Geckos are small lizards with a special talent, climbing. They can scale vertical walls, even windows, and they can scuttle upside down across ceilings. Many of them have have rounded pads at the tips of each toe. These pads spread out so the toes "stick" to surfaces.

Many geckos also make sounds. The tokay, the largest of all geckos, is named after its "to-kay" bark.

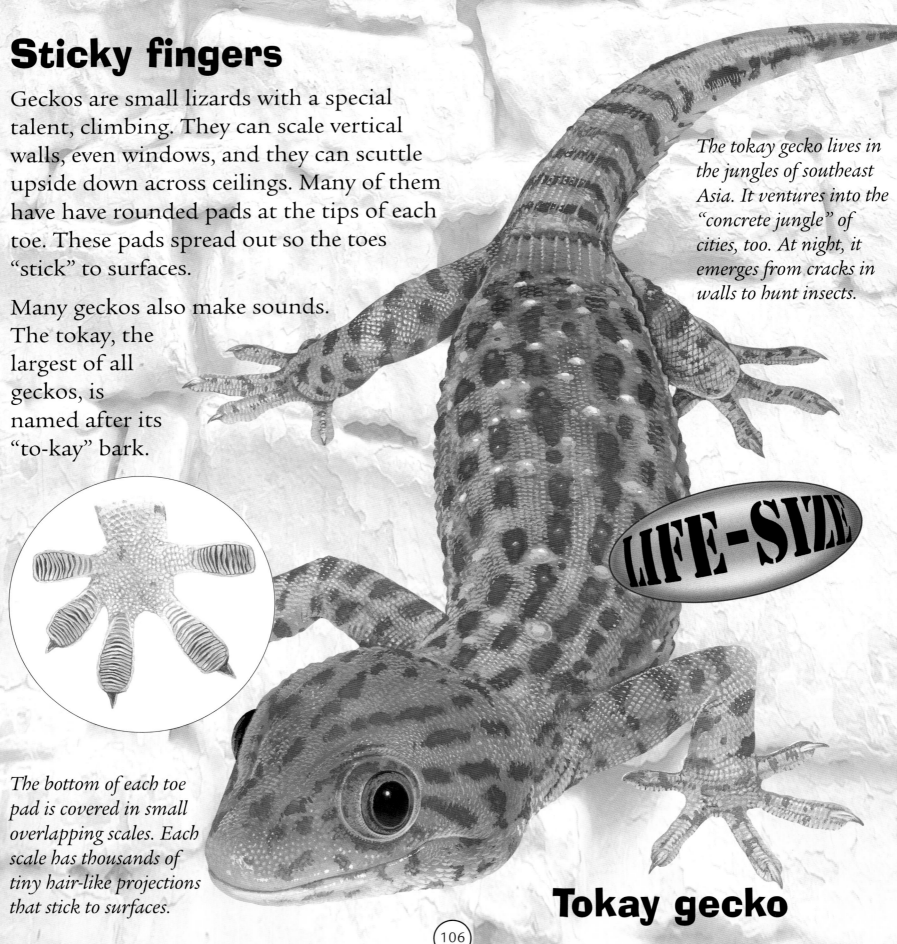

The tokay gecko lives in the jungles of southeast Asia. It ventures into the "concrete jungle" of cities, too. At night, it emerges from cracks in walls to hunt insects.

LIFE-SIZE

The bottom of each toe pad is covered in small overlapping scales. Each scale has thousands of tiny hair-like projections that stick to surfaces.

Tokay gecko

An ancient reptile

Tuataras may look just like lizards, but they're not. They are the last surviving members of a group of "wedge-toothed" reptiles that lived more than 200 million years ago. Unlike lizards, their teeth are fused to their jawbone and overhang at the front of the mouth to form a wedge shape. Today, they live only on a few islands in New Zealand. Tuataras rest by day, often in the old burrows of seabirds, and emerge at night to feed on beetles and spiders. Life progresses slowly for tuataras, it takes well over a year for this reptile to hatch from its egg and another 35 years to grow to full size!

The veiled chameleon has a high triangular-shaped skull, which helps to cool the lizard in the hot Middle Eastern climate. The head also funnels drops of dew toward its mouth, chameleons are fussy drinkers, preferring droplets to water from pools.

LIFE-SIZE

Veiled chameleon

A lizard of the ocean

The marine iguana of the Galápagos Islands in the Pacific Ocean is the only lizard truly adapted to an ocean life. With webbed feet and a powerful tail that acts like a rudder, this creature can swim beneath the waves, grazing on the plants and algae that cling to the rocky seabed. The lizards generally feed in shallow water and are under the water for about ten minutes at a time. Large iguanas can dive to a depth of 49 feet (15 meters) and stay underwater for more than an hour when they need to.

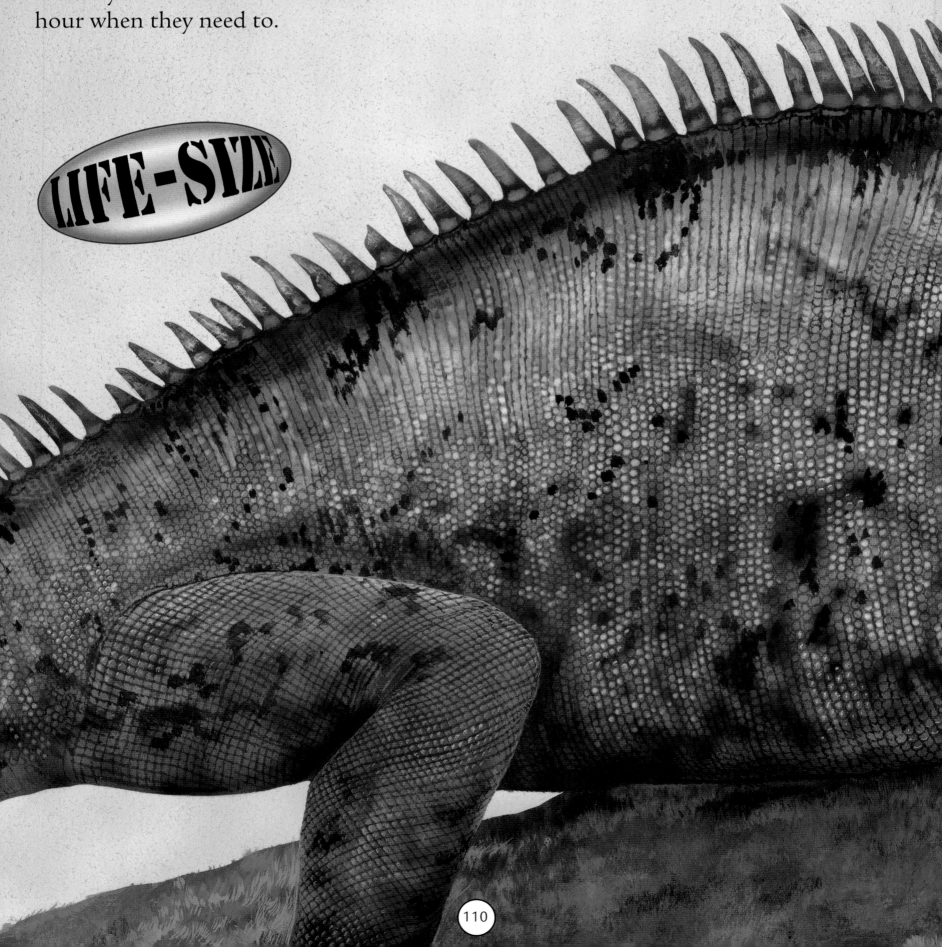

LIFE-SIZE

Tiny lizards

At only 16 millimeters long, the dwarf gecko is not just the smallest lizard, it is the smallest of all reptiles, birds, and mammals. Seen here at three times its actual size, the geckos live among the leaves on the forest floors of some Caribbean islands. Their habitat is under threat from deforestation, and their lives are not made easier by their size. Their tiny bodies cannot store much water, and the geckos risk drying out. And when you're not much bigger than an ant, many insects are predators rather than prey.

Nile monitor

Monitors can rear up on their hind legs, supported by their tail. They stand up to have a look around or to fight a rival.

Lizard kings

The largest lizards of all are the monitor lizards. And reaching 6.5 feet (2 meters) in length, the Nile monitor certainly measures up. This impressive creature is the largest African lizard. It is a strong swimmer and is never far from water. Its nostrils are positioned high on its snout so that it can breathe when swimming. The monitor uses sharp claws to kill the fish, crabs, and frogs in the water. It even braves attacks from mother crocs to steal eggs from their nests!

Tongues on target

The chameleon takes its time when hunting for a tasty insect. Clinging to a branch with its toes and tail, only its protruding eyes move, swiveling in different directions in search of a hopping cricket or a buzzing fly. Once the prey has been targeted, the chameleon shoots out its tongue, which can be longer than its body. The insect is ensnared by the tongue's sticky tip.

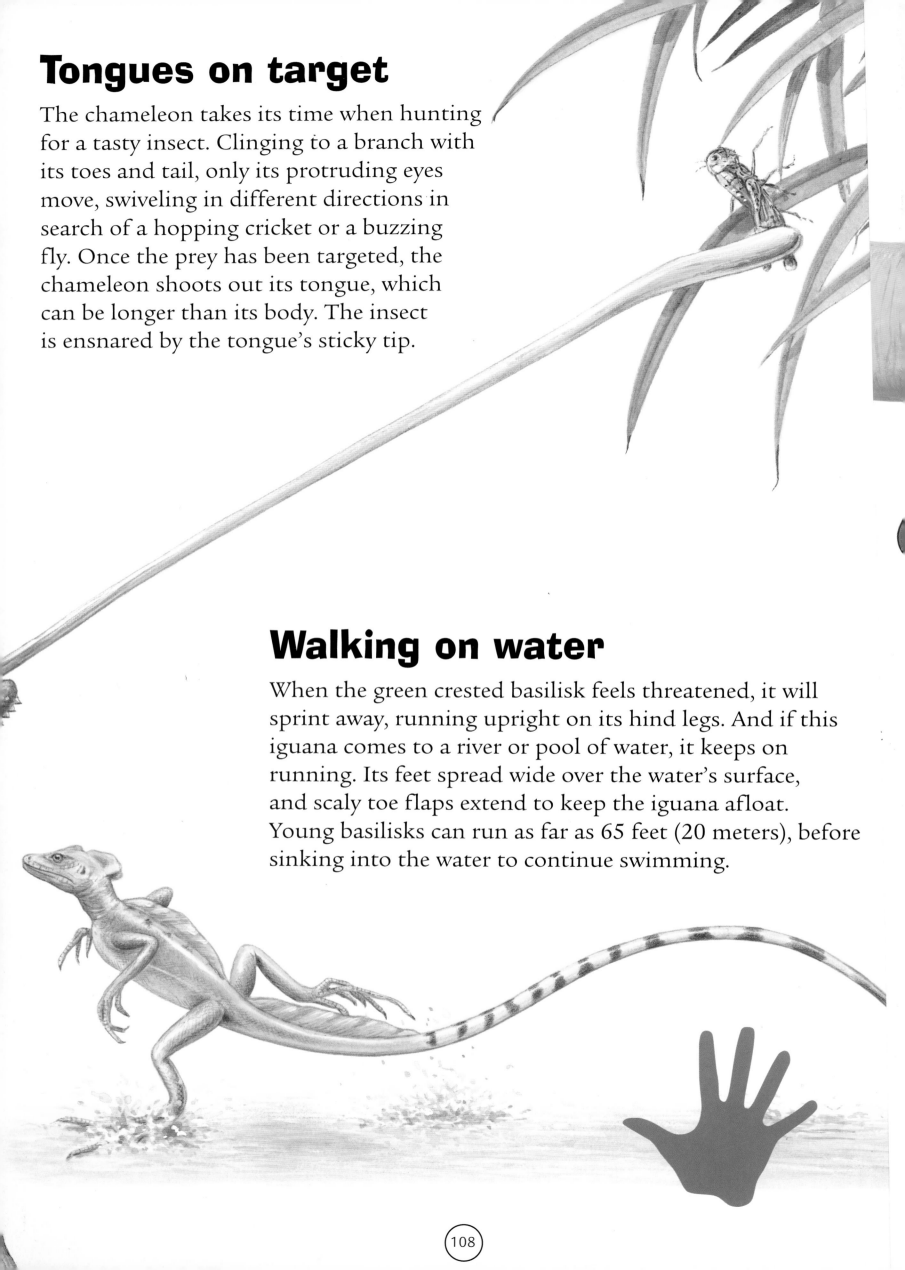

Walking on water

When the green crested basilisk feels threatened, it will sprint away, running upright on its hind legs. And if this iguana comes to a river or pool of water, it keeps on running. Its feet spread wide over the water's surface, and scaly toe flaps extend to keep the iguana afloat. Young basilisks can run as far as 65 feet (20 meters), before sinking into the water to continue swimming.

Color changes

When marine iguanas emerge from the cold ocean, their wet bodies are black. This helps them to absorb heat as they dry out in the sun on the rocky shoreline. They become paler after sunbathing. All marine iguanas have white-streaked faces, this is caused by the sea salt that they continually spray from their noses!

Marine iguana

Like many iguanas, this lizard has a spiky crest along its back. Males are larger than the females and grow to 4.3 feet (1.3 meters). When the males are ready to mate, their bodies develop colorful streaks.

A real-life dragon

More than 10 feet (3 meters) long and weighing up to 350 pounds, the Komodo dragon is a giant among lizards. On Komodo Island and the few other Indonesian islands that it inhabits, this monster is a fierce predator. It hunts pigs, goats, deer, and even kills buffaloes.

The dragon's spit contains a poison. This poison gets into the blood of prey when the lizard gives it a savage bite. If the prey escapes the first attack, the poison weakens it so it can't run far. The dragon tracks its dying victim, "smelling the air" by flicking out its huge forked tongue.

Like other monitor lizards, male komodos must fight for the right to mate with females. The lizards battle upright, standing on their hind legs. They slash at each other with sharp claws, and if one male turns away in retreat, he will do so with an aggressive thrash of a muscular tail.

Trunks and treetops

Many lizards are adapted to living among the trees of jungles and forests. They have "prehensile" tails that wrap around branches and feet built for gripping tree trunks. But the flying dragon doesn't bother with climbing for long jungle trips, it can glide between the treetops by extending flaps of skin that act like wings. The Australian frilled lizard also has flaps, but not for flying. In an impressively fierce display designed to scare off any hungry python, it opens a leathery frill around its neck, rocks backward and forward and hisses menacingly.

The bright pink gaping mouth and the orange frill – up to 1 foot (30 centimeters) wide, would startle any predator that moments before was facing a small brown lizard!

Frilled lizard

LIFE-SIZE

Desert dwellers

Lizards, like all reptiles, need to sunbathe to keep themselves warm, so life in hot, sunny deserts suits them well. Once they have reached their desired body temperature, the desert lizards climb trees in search of a cool breeze, seek shade in a rocky crevice, or simply lift their bodies as far above the hot sand as possible. Desert lizards don't drink. A diet of insects, often several thousand a day, provides the lizards with all the water they need.

Gila monster

The gila monster copes with the heat by emerging mainly at night. Covered with bead-like scales, it kills prey, such as rats or frogs, with a poisonous bite. It is one of only two species of lizard that are venomous.

The spines of the thorny devil help camouflage it among the stones of the Australian desert. And if the camouflage fails, predators are put off by such a spiky snack! Grooves between the spikes channel drops of moisture to the mouth, so the lizard does not waste any water.

Thorny devil

LIFE-SIZE

LIFE-SIZE

Komodo dragon

SNAKES

These strange fanged creatures, often with forked tongues, slit-like eyes and vivid colors, are unhindered by their lack of limbs. Snakes are masterful movers, silently slithering, climbing, burrowing, and even swimming through the world's warm regions.

LIFE-SIZE

Emerald tree boa

Snakes come in all shapes and sizes. Ground snakes are often short, heavy, and wide, whereas tree snakes, like this emerald tree boa, have long, slender bodies. Snakes' tails are more flexible than their bodies because they lack ribs. The tails of tree boas are prehensile, which means that they can grip onto branches.

Swimming snakes

The pelagic sea snake is one of the most venomous snakes of all, and its bright yellow belly warns sharks to keep away as it swims through the Pacific and Indian Oceans. This snake is perfectly adapted for an ocean life. Its tail is shaped like a paddle and it cannot move easily on land. Like marine iguanas, the snake cleans salt from its body, using glands under its tongue. The snake can remain underwater for more than three hours before returning to the surface to breathe. Often thousands of sea snakes drift together in a writhing mass of black and yellow scales.

Big mouths

Imagine trying to swallow something three times the size of your head. That is exactly what an egg-eating snake can do. Snakes can't chew food or rip it apart with claws so they must swallow it whole. Flexible jaws open wide, and elastic skin stretches over the egg, allowing it to pass through the throat into the stomach without ripping the snake apart. Anacondas and pythons perform the same trick but on a much larger scale, swallowing antelopes or even caimans whole. Snakes that eat such huge meals can go for weeks or months without eating again.

Blindsnake

The blindsnake cannot see at all. In fact, its skin has grown over its eyes completely. The snake has a smooth scale on its face that acts like a spade. Unlike other snakes, the blindsnake can't open its mouth wide, but this isn't a problem when tiny termites are on the menu.

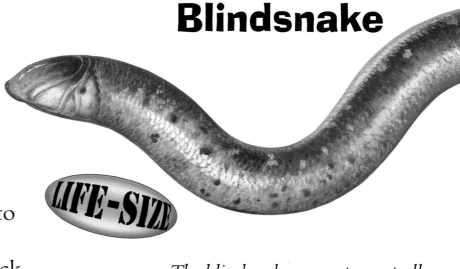

LIFE-SIZE

Egg-eating snake

Snakes great and small

There are 2,800 species of snake. They live across the world, from the chilly forests of Canada to the scorching deserts of Australia.

The largest snake in the world is the mighty green anaconda, which lives in the swamps and jungles of South America. Females are bigger than males and can grow to 33feet (10 meters) and weigh a quarter of ton! An anaconda does not bite its prey to death. Instead, the snake crushes its victim with its immense coils, squeezing so tightly that the prey cannot breathe. Large anacondas even kill other hunters such as caimans and jaguars. A hungry anaconda will also eat you if given the chance!

LIFE-SIZE

The smallest snake in the world is the Lesser-Antillean threadsnake, which could probably slither through a pencil if the lead was removed. This snake lives underground and is sometimes called the "worm snake".

Anacondas have many small, pointed teeth that hook onto prey as it is slowly swallowed. Prey might still be alive even as it is engulfed by the snake. But it cannot escape the snake's firm bite.

LIFE-SIZE

A sticky snout

The odd-looking leafnose vinesnake, from the island of Madagascar in the Indian Ocean, is a master of disguise. Its rough brown scales help the long, slender snake to resemble a twig. The female leafnose has another trick up its sleeve, or rather on its snout, a projection that looks just like a fir cone!

Warning rattle

The warning buzz of a rattlesnake's tail is a familiar sound in the deserts and scrubland of North America. The rattle is formed from scaly segments that do not fall off when the snake sheds its skin. The segments collect around the tip of the tail and rattle together when the snake shakes them. The rattle gets larger, and louder, every time this venomous viper sheds its skin.

Pits on the snake's face detect the body heat of prey.

The short rattle shows that this is a young snake.

Snakes might look as if they have no eyelids, but in fact both upper and lower sets are fused (joined together) to protect the eyes. The lids are made of transparent skin so the snakes can see through them.

Loose sand is a slippery surface, and desert snakes cannot push against it to move forward. Instead, many of them move with a motion known as sidewinding. The snakes lift sections of their bodies across the sand in a diagonal direction. The master of this movement is the sidewinder (left), a rattlesnake from North America.

④

③ Snakes can move by bunching their curved bodies together like an accordian and then stretching out again, so their bodies end up further forward. Tree snakes do this to reach across gaps between branches. Burrowing snakes move in a similar way, pushing their bodies against the walls of a tunnel.

The flying snakes of Southeast Asia cannot actually fly. Instead, they glide through the air and can travel 330 feet (100 meters) at a time as they leap from tree to tree. These snakes have flat bodies, and they spread their ribs to make a wing-like surface that catches the air.

Slither and slide

A snake's body is packed full of muscles and that makes it very strong yet flexible at the same time. Many snakes can even tie themselves in knots! Not having any legs does not stop snakes from getting around. They can twist, thrust and pull their bodies over or under ground, through trees, across deserts and even glide through the air. Snakes move in a number of ways, using different parts of their bodies to push themselves along.

Most snakes move by wriggling their bodies from side to side. This is called lateral undulation. Muscles contract on just one side of each section of the snake, and this creates S-shaped curves that move down the body like a wave. The curved body pushes against bumps on the ground to force the snake forward.

Heavy snakes like pythons move in a straight line, and it is often difficult to see how they do it. Sections of the body are lifted slightly off the ground. The scales left touching the ground hook onto the rough surface so the snake can heave itself along. This type of movement is slow but silent, and snakes use it when stalking prey.

Green anaconda

King of the snakes

If you annoy a king cobra, you'll probably regret it. The longest venomous snake in the world, reaching more than 16 feet (5 meters) in length, can rear up and look you straight in the eye. And if it gets really annoyed, it will flatten its upper ribs, creating a scaly hood, and hiss loudly. If that warning does not scare you away, the snake will strike, delivering a bite at incredible speed. The king cobra's venom is so powerful that it can kill an elephant in three hours. However, this Indian snake is more interested in catching its next meal, usually another snake!

LIFE-SIZE

Venomous fangs

Snakes inject venom into their prey to paralyze or kill it and make it easier to swallow. Venom is produced by glands in the jaw. When the snake bites, a muscle pumps the venom through a tube, or duct, toward the fangs. The venom then flows through hollows in the fangs or grooves on the outside. Spitting cobras spray clouds of venom from openings at the front of their fangs in an attempt to blind their prey. The most poisonous snake is the Australian taipan. The venom in a single bite could kill 100 people.

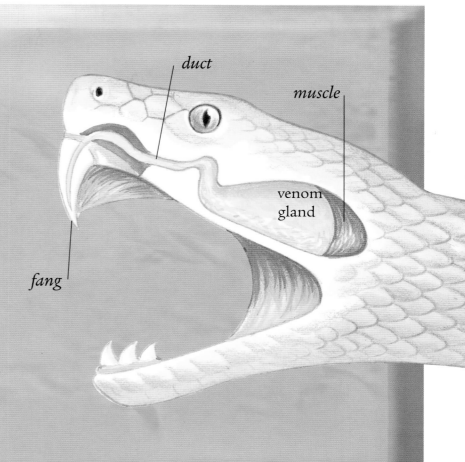

duct

muscle

venom gland

fang

Unlike many other snakes, the female king cobra builds a sophisticated nest. She piles up dead leaves and soil and creates a hollow for up to 50 eggs. Just before the eggs hatch, the cobra instinctively leaves the nest to prevent herself from eating her own offspring.

Saltwater crocodile

Ruler of the reptiles

The mightiest reptile on Earth, up to 26 feet (8 meters) in length and weighing more than a ton, is the ferocious saltwater crocodile. This beast is one of the animal kingdom's most dangerous predators and its favorite tactic is ambush. It lies in wait in the shallows of a river or swamp, only its eyes and nostrils are exposed above the water. If a buffalo comes for a drink, the croc will rush from the water and deliver a devastating bite. Its mighty jaws can snap antelope legs like twigs and crush turtle shells like crackers. The beast drags its prey back into the water and drowns it, often by spinning its victims underwater so they cannot struggle free.

CROCODILES

The largest reptiles on Earth are the fearsome crocodilians. These include the crocodiles, alligators, caimans and the strange-snouted gharial. With their long, toothy jaws, powerful tails, and tough armor plates, these carnivores are the rulers of their watery habitats.

The eyes, nostrils, and ears of this Cuban crocodile are at the top of the head so that they sit above the water. Unlike most reptiles, crocs have a third transparent eyelid that moves horizontally across the eye to protect it when the croc is underwater.

Ancient hunters

Crocodilians have survived unchanged since before the dinosaurs roamed the Earth. That is because crocs are perfect underwater killing machines. They paddle with webbed hind feet and use their powerful tail as a rudder. They can even eat fish or other prey underwater by closing a flap of skin in their throats to stop water from entering their lungs. But crocs don't just hunt in the water, the Cuban crocodile can leap completely out of a river to snatch a lizard from an overhanging branch.

Little and large

This baby American alligator may be small, but it still has sharp teeth and a strong jaw that can deliver a nasty bite. The alligator takes about ten years to grow to full adult size. By then the alligator will have lost its distinctive yellow bands because its skin will be coated with dark algae from its watery habitat. And it will reach 16 feet (5 meters) in length, that's pretty big for an alligator, which along with their relatives, the caimans, tend to be smaller than crocodiles.

LIFE-SIZE

Happy families

The Chinese alligator is very similar to the American alligator but is smaller, reaching no more than 6.5 feet (2 meters) long. Like all crocodilians, it is a good parent. The mother alligator is alerted to her newborns by their chorus of squeaks. She will dig the babies out of the muddy nest and carry them gently in her mouth to a safe place.

If the young alligators are struggling to get out of their shells, their mother will gently roll the eggs into her mouth to help crack them open.

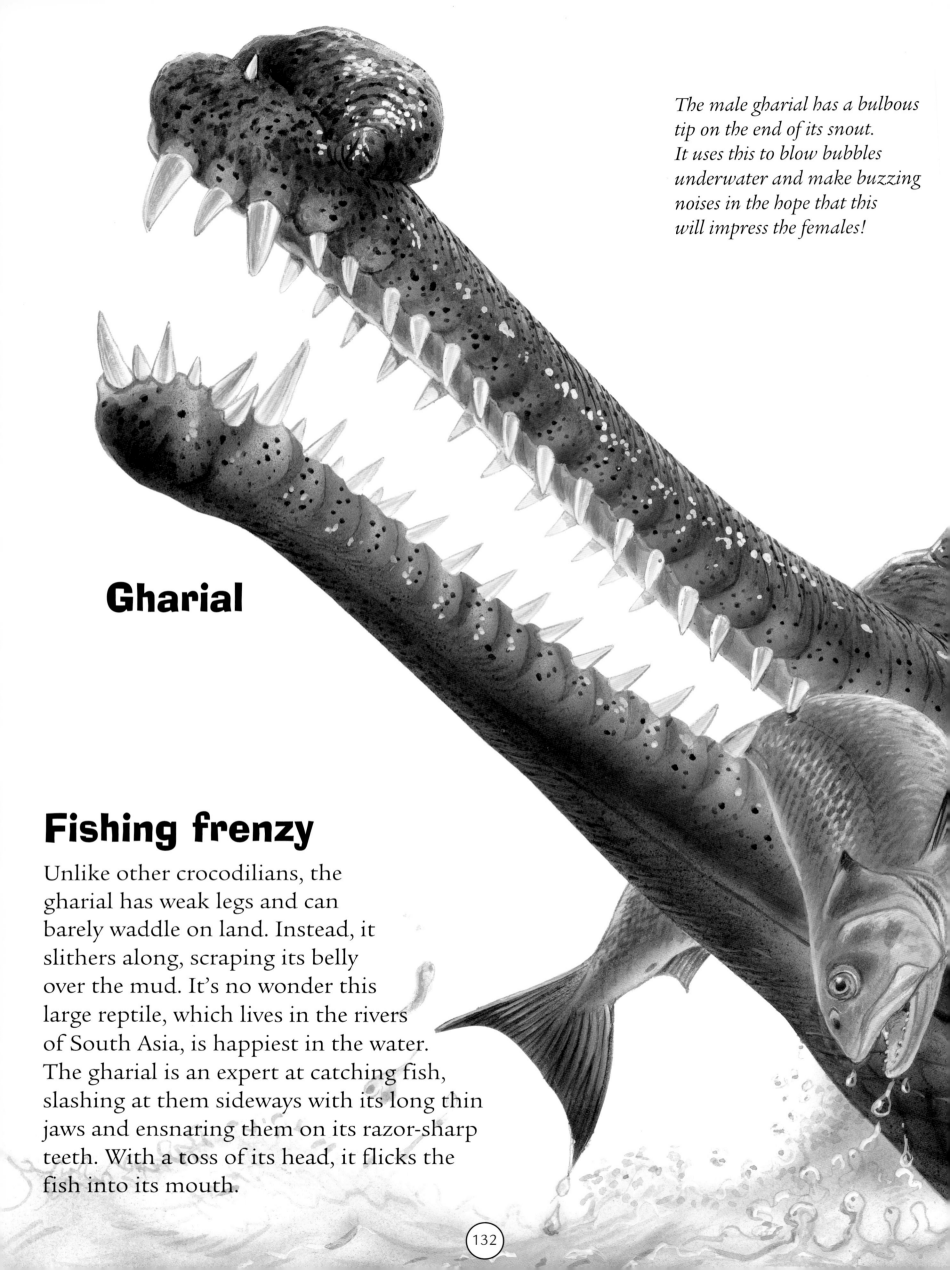

Gharial

The male gharial has a bulbous tip on the end of its snout. It uses this to blow bubbles underwater and make buzzing noises in the hope that this will impress the females!

Fishing frenzy

Unlike other crocodilians, the gharial has weak legs and can barely waddle on land. Instead, it slithers along, scraping its belly over the mud. It's no wonder this large reptile, which lives in the rivers of South Asia, is happiest in the water. The gharial is an expert at catching fish, slashing at them sideways with its long thin jaws and ensnaring them on its razor-sharp teeth. With a toss of its head, it flicks the fish into its mouth.

Toothy grins

The differences between the crocodilians can be observed by looking at their heads, and in particular their teeth. All crocodilians have at least 60 teeth and these are replaced many times throughout their life, one croc can get through as many as 3,000 teeth!

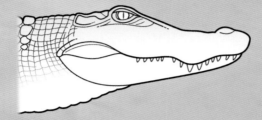

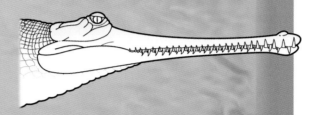

Crocodiles have long, V-shaped snouts. Both sets of teeth are exposed when their mouths are shut, giving crocs a toothy grin.

Alligators have shorter, rounded snouts. The upper jaw is wider than the lower one and covers the bottom teeth.

Gharials have very long and slender snouts with evenly spaced teeth that interconnect like a zipper.

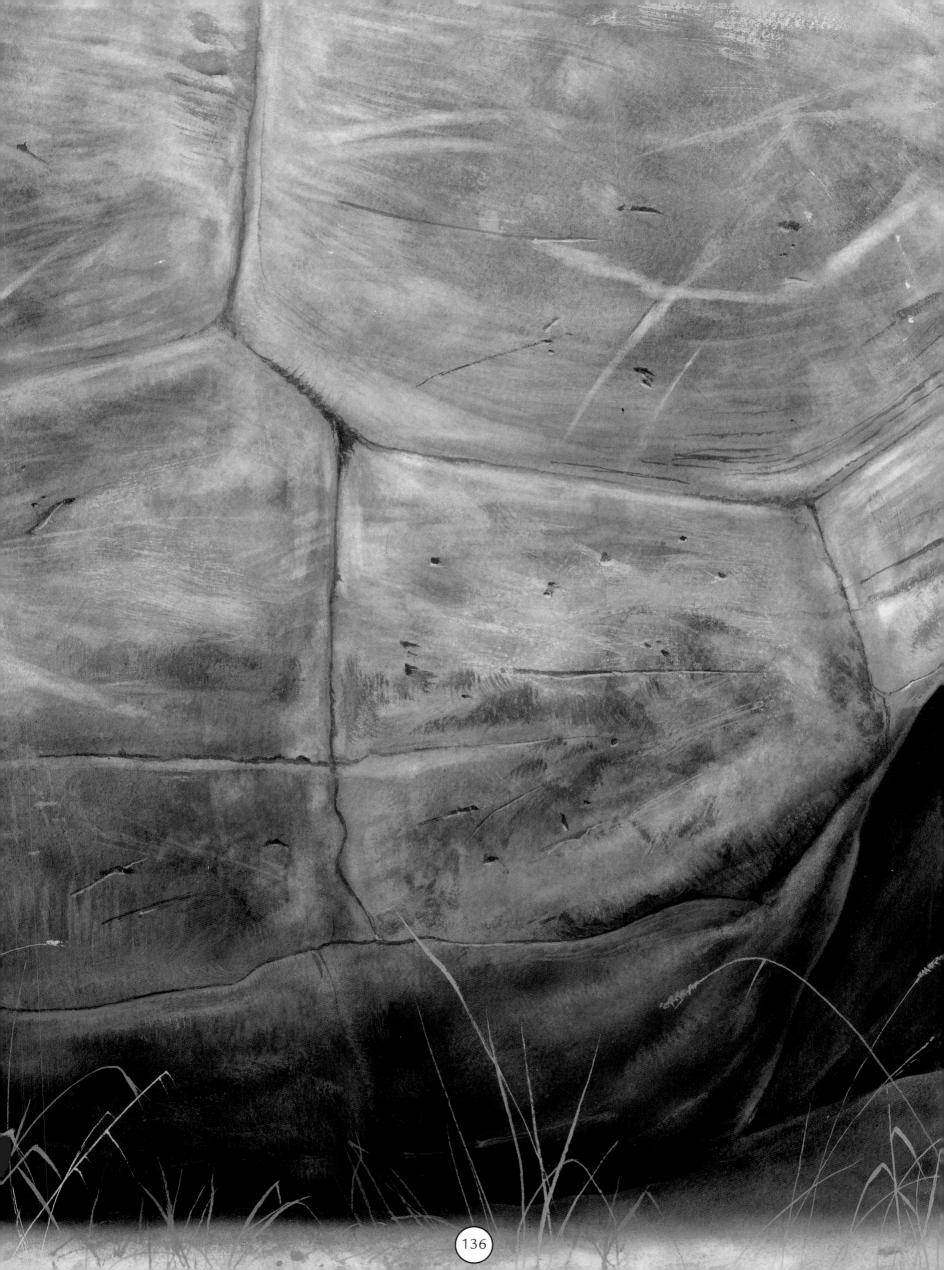

Gentle giant

This enormous scaly creature can weigh as much as an adult lion and live for 150 years. It lives its long, slow life on the Galápagos Islands in the Pacific Ocean, enjoying a morning sunbathe, followed by a search for a leafy meal and a snooze in a muddy hollow. The shape of a Galápagos tortoise shell depends on the habitat of the island where it lives. Tortoises that live on islands with low-lying vegetation have large, domed shells that prevent them from raising their heads upward. On other islands, tortoises have saddleback shells with a cut-out section behind the neck that allows them to reach up to munch on the leaves of taller plants.

TORTOISES AND TURTLES

Lumbering slowly over ground or swimming gracefully underwater, these largely sluggish reptiles are not the greatest hunters, often preferring to graze on vegetation on the forest or ocean floor. Tortoises and turtles may lack attack skills, but, with their armored shells, they're pretty good at defense.

Armored crawlers

Unlike turtles, which need smooth, flattened shells to slip through water easily, most tortoises have shells that are high and bumpy, a shape designed to put off any predator. The pancake tortoise uses a different defense tactic, its shell is flat. This allows it to fit into narrow crevices in its rocky African habitat.

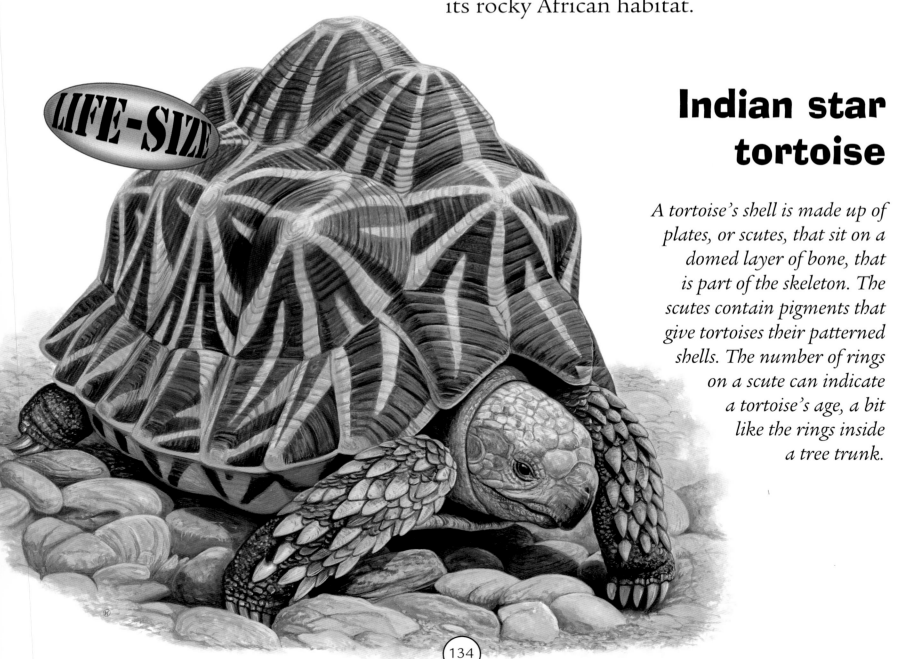

LIFE-SIZE

Indian star tortoise

A tortoise's shell is made up of plates, or scutes, that sit on a domed layer of bone, that is part of the skeleton. The scutes contain pigments that give tortoises their patterned shells. The number of rings on a scute can indicate a tortoise's age, a bit like the rings inside a tree trunk.

Ocean voyager

The leatherback is the largest turtle in the world, and one of the heaviest reptiles. It reaches about 8 feet (2.5 meters) in both length and width (with its flippers extended). It can weigh up to 1,750 pounds, the same as five komodo dragons. This enormous creature swims thousands of miles every year in search of jellyfish, which it catches with its hooked beak. The turtle takes its name from its supple leathery shell, which is lighter than the hard shells of other marine turtles.

Like all marine turtles, the leatherback has flippers (although uniquely, theirs are clawless). It doesn't need legs for walking like most freshwater turtles. Male leatherbacks never come on land and females spend just two hours ashore every few years, when they haul themselves onto a beach to lay eggs.

Giant
tortoise

Snorkeling snouts

Like all swimming reptiles, turtles must return to the surface of the water to breathe. The matamata of the Amazon, however, avoids this inconvenience by snorkeling. This weird-looking river turtle has a long tube-shaped snout with nostrils on the end. It pokes the snout above the water to take a breath. A river turtle from Australia goes to even further extremes to avoid surfacing, it breathes through its bottom! By pumping water into its backside, it can extract enough oxygen to stay underwater for three days.

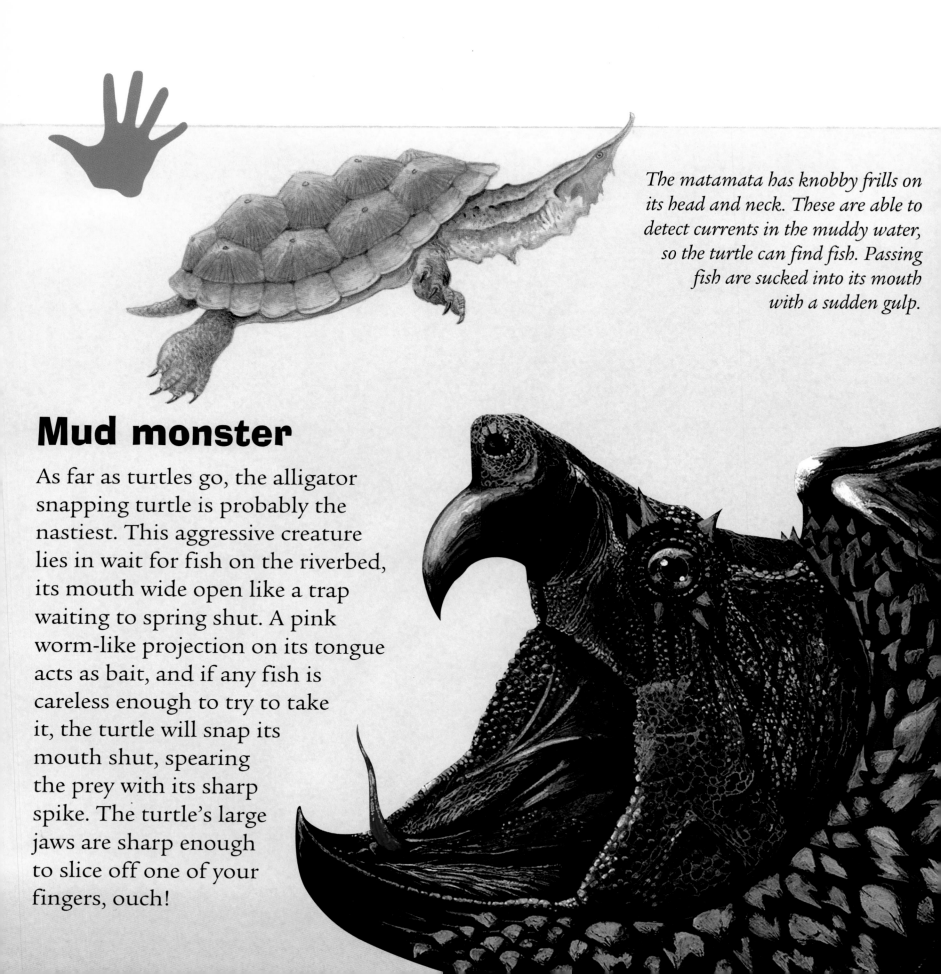

The matamata has knobby frills on its head and neck. These are able to detect currents in the muddy water, so the turtle can find fish. Passing fish are sucked into its mouth with a sudden gulp.

Mud monster

As far as turtles go, the alligator snapping turtle is probably the nastiest. This aggressive creature lies in wait for fish on the riverbed, its mouth wide open like a trap waiting to spring shut. A pink worm-like projection on its tongue acts as bait, and if any fish is careless enough to try to take it, the turtle will snap its mouth shut, spearing the prey with its sharp spike. The turtle's large jaws are sharp enough to slice off one of your fingers, ouch!

Taking cover

To take full advantage of their protective shells, most turtles and tortoises hide their heads inside them when danger is near. Different species take cover in different ways, and many can also withdraw their legs into their shells, too. However, a few turtles, such as the leatherback, cannot hide their heads at all.

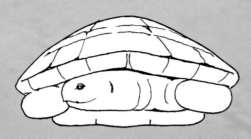

Tortoises and straight-necked turtles lower their heads and fold their necks into an S-shape under their spines. The head appears to move backward into the shell in a straight line.

Side-necked turtles have longer necks than the straight-necked species. They bend them to one side, hiding them under the lip of their shells.

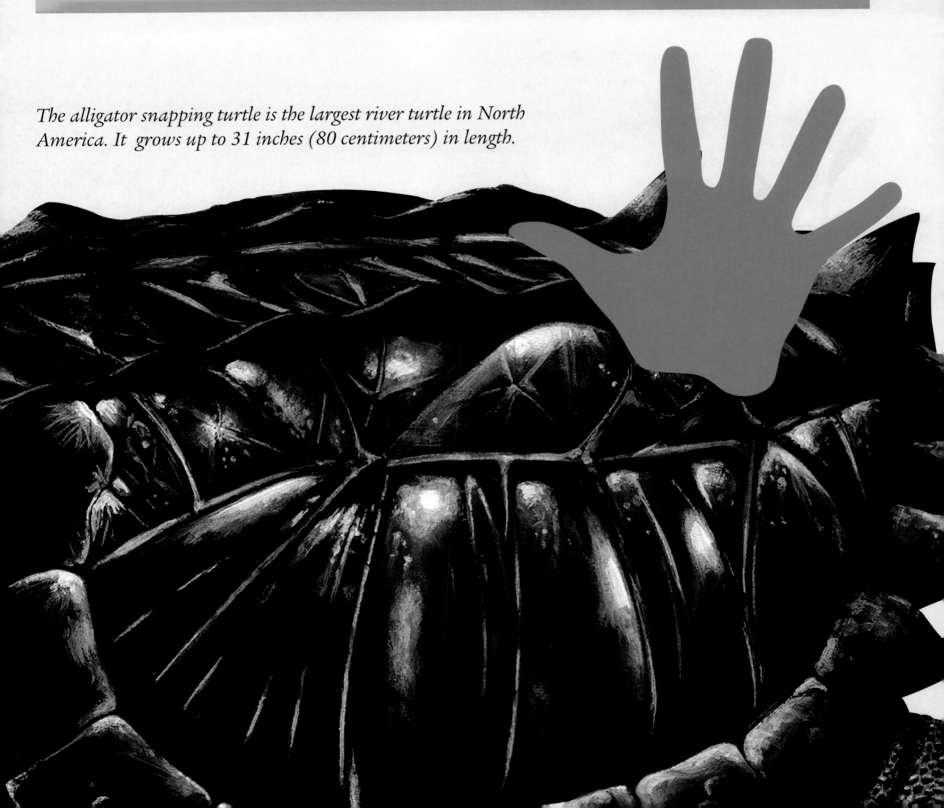

The alligator snapping turtle is the largest river turtle in North America. It grows up to 31 inches (80 centimeters) in length.

REPTILES AT RISK

The biggest threat to reptiles is humankind. Despite many protection laws, we still hunt them for food and for their skins, we capture them to sell as pets, and we destroy their habitats. If we don't stop, many of the species you have just read about, and more, will become extinct.

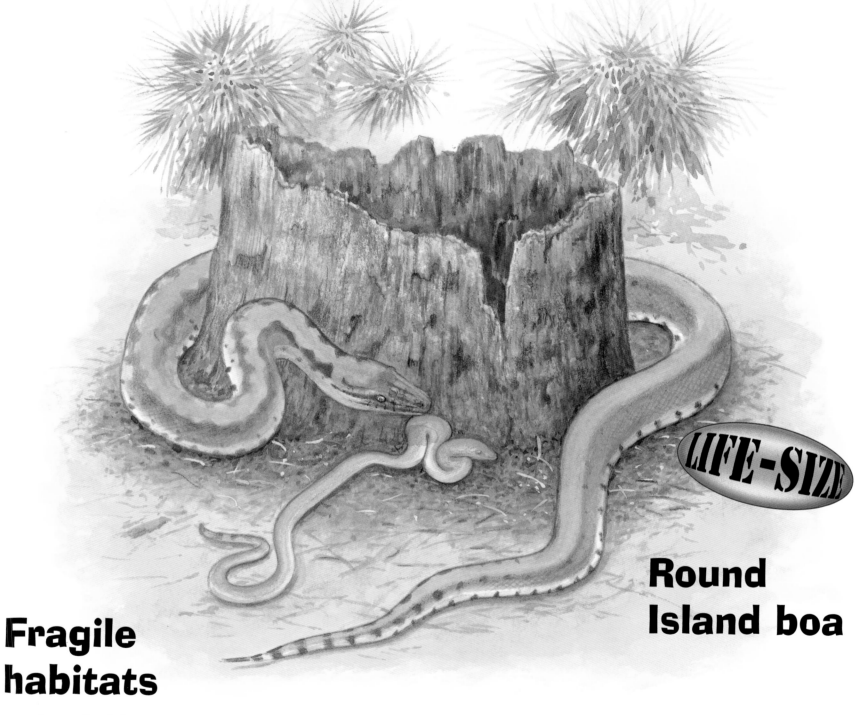

LIFE-SIZE

Round Island boa

Fragile habitats

Keel-scaled boas used to live on several islands in the Indian Ocean. They now survive on just one, tiny Round Island near Mauritius. The snakes died out elsewhere when rats were introduced to the islands. The boas were bred in zoos to boost their numbers, and their palm-forest habitat is protected. Nevertheless, they are still in danger of extinction.

When threatened, the armadillo lizard rolls itself up into a ball, gripping its tail firmly in its mouth. This pose protects its soft belly and presents an unappetizing spiky ring to a hungry eagle. However, it won't save the lizard from capture by someone hoping to sell it as part of the illegal pet trade.

Exotic pets

Reptiles have become popular pets, and the demand for rare or unusual creatures, like the spiny armadillo lizard from southern Africa, has led to a sharp decline in some populations. Up to 80 percent of caged reptiles do not survive the journeys to foreign pet stores. And, if the reptiles end up in non-expert hands, they very often become ill and die.

The ecological balance of the habitat these reptiles leave behind is also damaged. If too many snakes are taken from an area, the remaining mouse or rat population grows out of control. Reptiles are wild animals that need their natural habitats as much as their natural habitats need them.

Mysterious reptiles

The ajolote, or Mexican worm-lizard, is one of the strangest-looking reptiles of all. It is not actually a lizard and it's not a snake either. It's an amphisbaenian and is related to snakes and lizards, such as geckos and skinks. The worm-lizard has forelimbs at the front of its long, pink, ringed body, but no hind limbs. It lives underground, so we do not know much about its life. Although reptiles should not be kept as pets, it is important that scientists are able to study them so that we can understand and protect them and their environments.

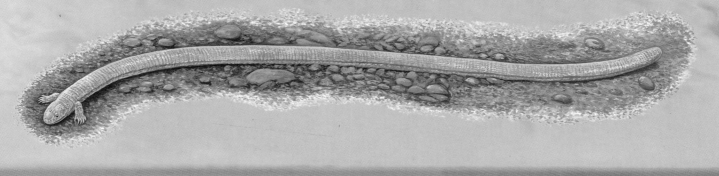

Vulnerable babies

Once the eggs are laid, the turtles' problems are not over. The tiny hatchlings have to dig themselves out of their sandy nest and then face a perilous dash across the beach to the ocean. Pulling themselves awkwardly over the sand with their tiny flippers, the hatchlings are helpless if preyed upon by crabs, gulls, or lizards.

Hawksbill turtle

The female hawksbill turtle digs a deep burrow with her back flippers. After laying up to 200 eggs, she covers them with sand and returns to the ocean. After about two months, the tiny hatchlings emerge and head for the sea. They are probably guided by the reflection of the moon and stars on the water's surface. Lights from buildings near the shore can confuse the turtles, preventing them from reaching the ocean.

Coming ashore

All sea turtles are endangered. They are hunted for food and for their shells, which are used to make jewelry. Female sea turtles must also take a risk when coming ashore to lay eggs. They prefer to make their nests on long, sandy beaches, but that is also where humans like to spend their holidays. Too many people on a beach will scare the turtles away, and many can't find a place for their eggs.

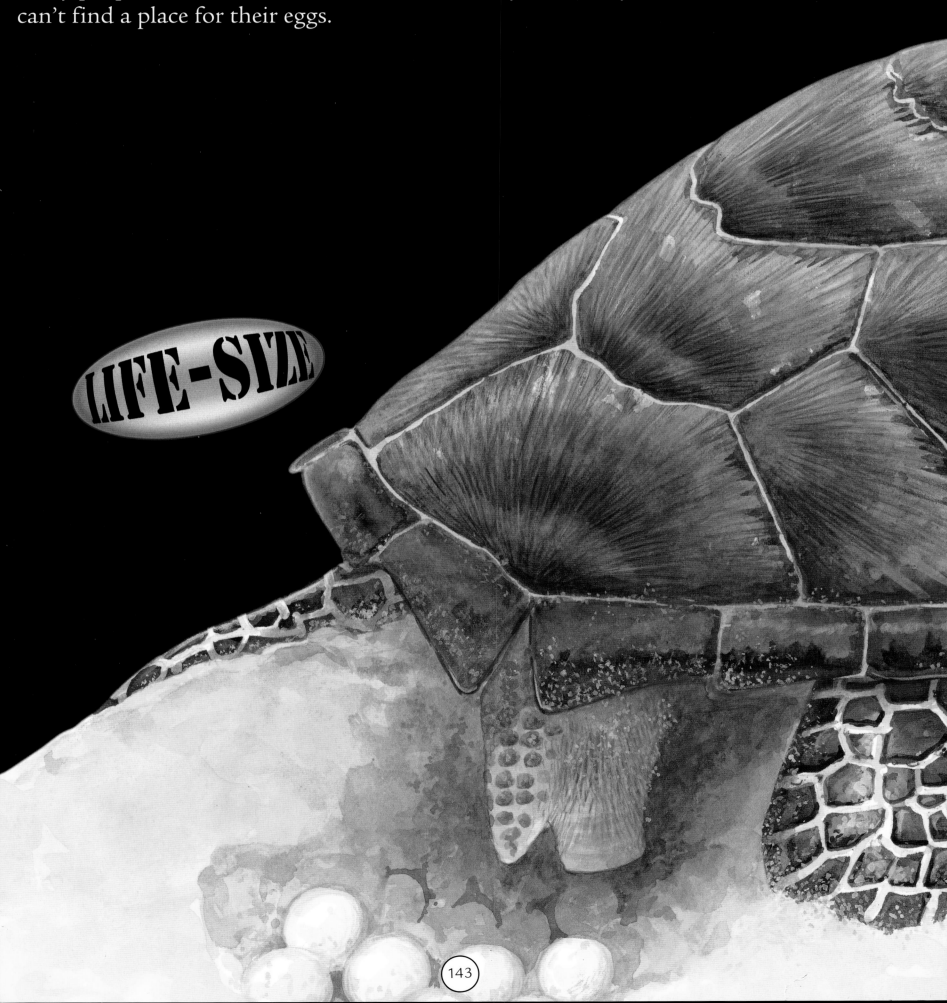

LIFE-SIZE

INDEX

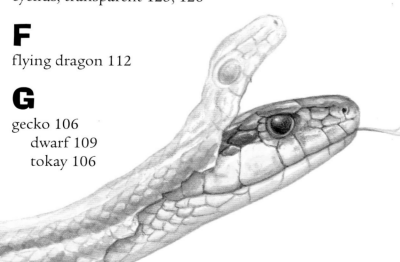